TWO POETS

A
Special Collection
of
Original Poetry

Vandaver Boling, Jr.

Two Poets

Rex B. Valentine

*Their Lives from Poor Farm Boys
to
Distinguished American Poets*

Illustrated by Rex B. Valentine

All rights reserved.

No part of this book may be reproduced or transmitted in any form or by any means, electronic or mechanical, including photocopying, recording, or by any information storage and retrieval system, without permission in writing from Rex B. Valentine.

This book was printed in the United States of America.

Copyright©2015 by Rex B. Valentine

Illustrated by Rex B. Valentine

ISBN 978-0-692-32445-5

To order more copies of this book contact: Rex B. Valentine at *rexvalentine@yahoo.com*

or on his website *www.rexbvalentine.com*

~ CONTENTS ~

The Poetry of Vandaver Boling, Jr.

PHOTOS OF VANDAVER BOLING, JR. 1	TREE PLANTERS 62
VANDAVER BOLING, JR. 7	SCOTTY. 63
IN CONFIDENCE. 14	RED MURPHY 64
FIRESIDE. 14	NIGHT WHISTLE. 67
FOREST, FIELD AND STREAM 15	ON THE OLD, OLD SUBJECT 68
A GRAY HAIRED BOY 16	THE GREEDY PIGGY 69
FOUR-LEAFED CLOVER. 17	THOSE FRESHIE BOYS. 70
WANDERERS. 18	MINUET IN G. 70
TO OUR CHILDREN. 19	THE BUILDER 71
TIME. 19	MY PUPPY 72
WHAT WILL MOTHER SAY?. 20	GOOD-NIGHT. 73
WHEN COW BELLS PEAL. 21	KEEP HOPIN'. 74
THE MAN IN OVERALLS 22	A TRAGEDY (APOLOGIES TO POE) 75
THE PRIZE WINNER 23	AT HOME TO-NIGHT. 76
THE WORTHY ONE. 24	AWAKEN THE BOY 77
PAUL BUNYAN'S BOYS 25	THE QUESTION BOX. 77
ROOTS 27	GRANDMA 78
CROCUS 27	THE DEEPEST SILENCE. 79
CHILDREN 28	THE TRICKSTER 80
MY MOTHER. 28	SELL OUT 80
TEA KETTLES. 29	A BROWNIE'S EXPERIENCE. 81
THE WREN 29	DAVY JONES 82
THOSE LITTLE SHOES. 30	ELMA 83
WHEN DADDY COMES HOME. 31	WHAT THE FIR TREE SAID 84
SHAMROCK 32	TO A KITTEN 84
BEAUTIFUL CHEHALIS 32	EASILY MISTAKEN. 85
AN ARGUMENT 33	PROCRASTINATION 85
HOOSIER LAND 34	HALLOW-E'EN. 86
HE PLANTED A TREE. 35	A WIFE'S MONOLOGUE. 87
IN THE MORNING. 36	WHAT MIND THE RAIN? 88
IT'S OVER NOW. 37	TOGETHER AGAIN 89
THE SUN TO BED 38	DON'T FORGET YOUR SIRE. 90
SIEGE OF DARKNESS. 39	SYMPATHY 91
TALE OF THE DESERT 40	THE LITTLE TYKE 92
THE DAY IS OLD 46	MEDITATION 92
ON TO OREGON 47	BELL SONG 93
MANY A TIME 48	IT CAN'T BE DONE 94
LECTURE NUMBER ONE. 49	SPRING 94
WISDOM 49	THE BURIAL OF ANSEL TRINE 95
A BACHELOR'S SOLILOQUY 50	THE VANISHING FOREST 96
TOOLS. 51	COMPANIONS. 102
WESTPORT 52	AT GETTYSBURG 103
YOUTH AND I 53	HUNTERS 104
A BED TIME TALE 54	THAT WORD GOOD-BYE. 104
DROUGHT 56	CROSSING THE DELAWARE 105
DREAMS 57	LINES ON BURNS 106
GOLDEN WEDDING ANNIVERSARY 58	THE DOUBLE CROSS. 107
WHEN DROPS THE VEIL 59	TIDE IN, TIDE OUT .108
CHILD EXPERTS 59	UNDERSTANDING .109
SEALED LIPS 60	WE CAN! WE WILL! WE MUST!. 110
THE SCOUT 60	MY OLD HOME TOWN 111
SURE IT'S SINGING 61	HOMESICKNESS 112

The Poetry of Rex B. Valentine

THE POETRY OF REX B. VALENTINE 115	SUMMER SCENES FROM OUR TEENS 221
PHOTO GALLERY OF REX B. VALENTINE. . .120-122	THE WILD STEER HUNT 227
REX B. VALENTINE 123	THE VALENTINE ADVENTURE 232
WISDOM. 126	THE GRANDEST GRANDKIDS 233
THE MAN I WANT TO BE 127	BILLIE JEAN. 236
PRESERVE BEAUTY 128	BE MY GUEST 237
RE-RUNS IN THE THEATRE OF LIFE 129	SLIPPING FROM WORK TO REST. 238
LEARNING TO MILK EVANGELINE 130	DEAR AUNTIE IS OLDER 239
FIRST THE FIGHT AND THEN THE RIGHT 131	COUSIN DICK AND THE RIVER'S PERIL. 240
A DOG NAMED BOB .136	CEDAR CREEK, THE ENCHANTED STREAM . . .242
OUR FAIR FEATHERED FRIENDS IN FLIGHT . . .138	THE MODEL T FORD. 243
HINDSIGHT 139	THE MASTER MIND .246
LEADERSHIP. 139	THE SIMPLE PRAYER. 247
PERSISTANCE 139	WHERE IS PEACE? 247
ROVIN' WITH ROVER. 140	THE TIP. 248
SEARCH FOR THE GOLD. 142	THE WONDER OF LOVE 250
I AM AN AUTHORITY 143	THE DRINKING CONTEST 251
THOSE FOOTBALL FEELINGS 144	THE BEAUTY OF A WAVE. 253
THE RUTABAGA PATCH 149	THE ADDRESS BOOK. 254
WILDFLOWERS AND LOVE 153	THANKSGIVING IN JUNE 255
CINDERFELLA. 154	THE MEDICARE BAND AT THE NURSING HOME 260
A SINNER'S LAMENT .162	THE PRUNER. 263
MILKING THE COWS. 163	THE BOUQUET OF LIFE 264
OPEN DOORS 164	THE DAY WE RANG THE BELL. 265
PLAN FOR SUCCESS .165	SPREADING CHESTNUT WISDOM 271
A LESSON OF LIFE. 165	A BLOSSOM OF SPRING. 273
HAIRWAYS, OR THE HAIRPECKED HUSBAND 169	ART OF LIFE, DANCE OF PEACE. 274
EXPECTATION 171	THE MISTIC MEADOW 274
COUSIN DICK AND THE BEAR. 172	COMING HOME 275
ESCAPE THE HONEY DOOS. 175	IN MY HEART I'M DANCING 276
WHO WERE THOSE WHO KEPT THE FAITH? . . .176	
AUSTRALIAN HSINKU. 178	
FROG HSINKU 178	
WHY HIS SONG WAS LONG. 178	
GOODBYE OLD FRIENDS 179	
MY MIND, A MINE 180	
GATOR 181	
PRECIOUS WATER. 182	
OUR OLD FARMHOUSE SLEEPING PORCH 183	
A MIDNIGHT VISITOR. 185	
DESSERT FIRST. 188	
FIRST & LAST KISS LIGHTNING STRIKES TWICE 189	
FROM BELT TO SUSPENDERS 192	
TOMMY. 193	
WHAT HAPPENED TO THE STUMPS 198	
THE PARADIGM OF A FENCE. 202	
THE HOUSE WITH A PURPLE DOOR 204	
THE HAMMER AND THE AXE 205	
THE CHRISTMAS FOOTBALL WISH. 207	
THE SKUNK TRAPPERS 212	
THE CEDAR FOREST .216	
THANKSGIVING DAY 219	
PERFECT COMMUNICATION 220	

Dedication

~ On Behalf of Van ~

This poetry book is dedicated to the Boling family and descendants of Vandaver Boling, Jr. May they always keep and reserve his special place expressed in his stories and poetry of his home community of Elma, WA, where he lived his entire life. His wonderful writings capture everyday happenings from an unusual prospective and his uncanny ability to describe with words, his heartfelt mental pictures and feelings are in a class few authors ever achieve.

Aknowledgment

~ On Behalf of Van ~

Vandaver Boling Jr, although deceased 60 years prior to this publication, would credit this revival of his excellent poetry to the Boling family whose progeny wants to see his work received by more people who can appreciate the beauty of his life and the special spirit that permeates his carefully written pages. Also, Rex B Valentine has dedicated much effort to help perpetuate Van Boling's special contribution to the World of Poetry.

*Vandaver Boling, Jr., as a teenager.
Student Body President of Elma High School.*

EHS Football Squad 1917

Van outside his house with his saxophone. Van loved playing and writing music.

Van with his daughter Margaret, whom everyone called Peggy.

Van Boling bucking timber (cutting it into smaller lengths)

Vandaver Boling Jr., right, a woodsman, resting while falling a large tree.

Van as a young man,

*as well as a grown man
and established poet.*

(Photo by Charles Kerr, World Staff.)

HARBORITE TURNS POET: Van Boling, native born Elma verse writer, glances through his most recently published book of poems. The book, called "Fireside" cost Boling hundereds of hours of work. Themes of the poems are largely drawn from his observations during the years he spent as a log bucker and mill-hand.

In his later years, Van studied the works of world renowned poets.

VANDAVER BOLING, JR.

Vandaver "Van" Boling, Jr. was born in the Greenwood District of Elma, Chehalis County, Washington on October 29th, 1901 and died at the Elma Hospital on the 15th of September, 1954 just before the hospital was closed. His parents were Vandaver Boling, Sr. and Mary Catherine Olive (Johnson) Boling.

Van had three brothers and three sisters, Leon, Daws, Chet, Florida Trombley, Lula Winslow and Laura Allan. Together, along with their parents, they lived on the old C.C. Combes ranch East of Elma. It was located on the straight stretch between Elma and Malone and is where Van was born. He, no doubt, was a special, serious child. From what others recalled he educated himself, having a great desire to learn as much as possible in school and in his everyday experiences as an adult. He evidently wanted to go on to college, but spent his education savings to help a sister who was ill.

Van was very active in school and loved to read and write poetry. He studied the poems of some of the great master poets, including Tennyson and Longfellow, developing his beautiful style of writing so the reader fell into the spirit of his poems and could experience the descriptive scenes of beauty or of action, and did not want them to end.

Back in his school days several pictures show him with his beloved saxophone. He played in the Elma High School Orchestra and smaller groups. Music was in his soul and as he matured he published several songs and was honored for his work. One of the songs he wrote the lyrics for was published in 1943 by Santly Joy Inc. The music was written by Sam H Stept and entitled "You're The Keeper Of My Heart." At the age of 42 Van got some good recognition for his work and was paid a few dollars. During this time the 2nd World War was going on, so the theme of the song asked the woman to "keep his heart" while he was away, implying he was going to fight for his country in another land. He also wrote and published the lyrics for "Give Your Tomorrows to Me."

In high school he wrote many rhymes and limericks about his friends and what he experienced. He was Editor in Chief of the monthly school publication and for several years was either the Editor or Assistant Editor of the Elma High School Yearbook, called the "Valley Echo." In the 1919, 1920, and 1921 editions, there are many stories, poems, and articles written by him. Van had a good grasp of the English language and seemed to use colorful colloquial expressions mixed with more normal phrases to describe his subjects, their antics, feelings, and activities. He had great diversification of subject matter; a good vocabulary, and has produced a homey tang that often strikes the heart chords. This rendered much of his poetry unique and equal to other great poets of the 20th Century. His explanations of things brought a fresh perspective to a situation or subject. His writings also indicate he had a good sense of humor.

Van was Student Body President of Elma High School his Senior Year, and enjoyed the debating team for four years, of which he was also President. It mentions in the 1921 school yearbook that "he has a face like a benediction," emphasizing his studious, serious demeanor. Van loved sports and was the reporter for the football and basketball teams, and shows up in the team football picture of 1917, his freshman year. (Photo located on page 2)

As an adult he married Bernice Margaret Hjelm in 1925. His family soon came along, a boy and three girls (Kenneth, Shirley, Marguerite and Judy), who were very dear to him. Some of his poems describe his interactions with his children throughout their growing up years.

Van worked in the woods as what is known as a "log bucker"; although he also did some falling of the trees and other logger tasks. The log bucker's main job was to cut the fallen trees into logs of proper size and cut off their limbs before they were taken to the mill to be cut up into dimensional lumber for building. Log bucking was a tiresome job when done with the great effort of trying to maximize production for time spent. Trees usually fell into and over rough ground making it a great effort to carry the long cross-cut saw, axe, and other tools through the maze of fallen trees with many broken and bent branches mixed with brush on the ground. When he first started his job, the big saw only worked with his muscles as he drew it back and forth severing the huge logs. Later Van was introduced to the power saw whose engine ran on gasoline. It did the job much faster if he could keep it running, but the danger of the flashing saw blade and the heavy weight of the saw injured many buckers. The saw he used weighed from 50-60 lbs and was a real chore to carry all day along with his axe and other equipment. After being a log bucker Van worked in a saw-mill, cutting up logs like the ones he had bucked into dimensional lumber. It is said by the family that Van's cancer started from a sore on his right shoulder from carrying his axe and saw so many miles. In an effort to save him the Doctors amputated his right arm and shoulder. He wrote left handed for his remaining time, but finally succumbed and the great poet's heart was stilled.

This information was taken from various articles published in the Mc-Cleary Observer, The Aberdeen World (The Daily World), The San Diego Union and The Elma Chronicle. Some material was presented by Randy Beerbower, including the photos, Eileen Boling, and others. Van's poems have been taken from various Elma High School Year Books, The 1919, 1920, and 1921 Valley Echoes, his first book "Fireside Verse" published in 1940 and his second book "Fireside" published in 1952, about two years before his death.

Mr. Valentine came upon Vandaver's two little soft back books of poetry published over 50 years ago by trading one of his books for one of Van's books still held by his son Kenneth Boling. Mr. Valentine was so impressed with Van's work he negotiated with Van's heirs to republish a collection of his work along with a special collection of Valentine's poems which he was getting ready to publish anyway, to assure that Boling's works will be available to a larger number of people, and hopefully Van Boling will receive his due as one of the greatest of all American poets. Permission was given to Rex B Valentine by Van's grandson Thomas V Boling on November 2, 2007.

Once permission was given Rex began to research Van and compiled all the information he could find and included it in this publication. It was then that he realized the many similarities in their lives, though they were raised about 20 miles and 33 years apart.

Both were born on primitive farms: Boling October 19, 1901 at Greenwood near Elma, and Valentine February 7, 1934 in the Wynooche Valley North of Montesano. They both learned to work horses, milk and take care of cows and raise pigs and chickens. Both enjoyed sports at school, including football, and worked on their schools' newspapers as sports reporters. Each one worked on their school yearbooks writing poems and articles, as well. The similarities don't end there, both men were Student Body Presidents in their schools. When Boling was President of his high school debate team, one session had the subject "Resolved that as a prerequisite to strikes and lockouts, Employers and Employees should submit Industrial Disputes to Arbitration, the machinery for which shall be furnished by the National Government." This showed Vans interest in and concern for the actions of labor unions. Valentine also was concerned about the same basic problem 31 years later. His Valedictorian address at commencement discussed the coming abuses of labor unions with their lack of checks and balances.

Also, both played the saxophone, published original music, peeled cascara bark, bucked timber in the woods and published poetry books. They both served their community in many ways, Boling served the Elma Community as Police Commissioner for awhile and also served on Elma's City Council in 1950, 1951, & 1952. Whereas Valentine was appointed a member of the first Elma Planning Commission at a later date and served 11 years helping zone the entire town, and four years on the Grays Harbor County Library Board, and eight years on the Grays Harbor Shorelines Board (4 years as Chairman). Their goals seemed to be similar in many respects. Their families' comfort and care being first on their lists. Both found solace in expressing life through poetry.

THE POETRY OF

Vandaver Boling, Jr.

IN CONFIDENCE

Within this book I hope you find
Some merit here and there;
Some little thought that strikes you kind,
That you will say is fair.

And when these pages you have scanned,
I hope that you'll incline
To want to shake me by the hand,
And be a friend of mine.

FIRESIDE

Deep in my old armchair
Here by the fire alone,
Watching the cheery flare,
Cozy world of my own.

Swiftly the flames leap high
Slowly the wood burns low.
Crackle, and sizzle, and sigh,
Sparkle and ruddily glow.

Shadows upon the wall
Dance as the sprites at play,
Silently rise and fall,
Noiselessly fade away.

Embers of living red,
Ashes they soon will be;
Past time to go to bed
Still I sit hungrily.

Wooed by the voice of sleep,
Imp that must coax and fawn,
Thoughts from the nameless deep
Linger and then are gone.

Here let me grandly dream,
Here let my ego shine;
Here life and love supreme,
One little realm, all mine.

FOREST, FIELD AND STREAM

There are sights out in the forest
                That will fill a man with awe;
From the strongest to the fairest—
                All obey the primal law.
There the weak ones must be fleetest,
                For the strong roam wide at will;
The survival of the fittest—
                Ancient codes are used there still.
Have you seen swift judgment grim
In some woodland recess dim?

In the meadow, while out walking,
                Have you heard the wee folk chat?
Always and forever talking,
                Arguing, on this and that?
Seen a mother rise in anger,
                Driven reckless by the fear
That her young are facing danger—
                That an enemy is near?
Have you seen such love revealed
By shy people of the field?

Have you dozed by brook a-winding,
                Listened to the bluejays jibe;
Sat there creeping hours unending,
                While you watched the finny tribe?
Have you seen them dart in hiding
                At some unaccustomed sound;
Seen them catch the flies confiding
                When the shadows gather 'round?
Have you watched the darting gleam
Of sly people of the stream?

If you've seen the things I mention,
                Then you know that they exist;
If unclaimed by your attention,
           What a precious page you've missed!
Don't be slave to hesitation—
                Take the day and come with me!
Out there lies an education
                We all need and wholly free.
Lives of nature's own revealed,
                Of the forest, stream and field.

A GRAY HAIRED BOY

To me, no one deserves more praise
Than he, who in his waning days—
Although his hair is sparse and gray,
Can always view in calm, clear way,
This life which oftentimes brings sorrow
And heavy cares; who will not borrow
One trouble in its mildest sense:
Who laughs and cries, "Life is immense!"
Can mole hill from a mountain tell;
Though clouds hang low, know all is well.
Who feels each added day is blest,
Is sweeter, grander than the rest;
Who has a jovial gift of tongue
Is, down inside, forever young!

And such a man we should admire—
He doesn't sit up near the fire
Complaining on the ways of fate,
Or moaning that it is too late
To do the things he longed to do.
For such a man has twisted view;
We pity him—sad is his lot,
We pity him—but envy not!
When I am old and gray and bent,
Though all the cares of man be sent,
I hope that I may bear them all
With cheerful grace, no curses call
On life, or love, or those who sing.
May I join in and help them bring
More joy to earth, more happiness,
More smiling and less wistfulness;
There's nothing that I'd more enjoy
Than being called a "gray haired boy!"

FOUR-LEAFED CLOVER

Did you ever go down in the orchard so cool,

In summer, when kids aren't bothered with school,

There crawl on your knees in the heavenly shade,

While you anxiously searched through each blossom and blade,

With the keen hope of finding a talisman hid,

A rare four-leafed clover that's luck to a kid?

            I did!

Do you know the grand glow that a clover can bring?

It makes a boy feel like a genuine king.

For good luck is something that every boy craves,

So he picks all the "luckies" and carefully saves,

And he never would sell them whatever the bid.

Did you save four-leafed clovers when you were a kid?

            I did!

Though you may be getting a little bit gray,

With work that grows tiresome day after day.

Would you visit an orchard and under the trees,

Look all through the clovers, on hands, and on knees;

Prospect for a "lucky" an hour or two,

And really enjoy it the way that boys do?

           I would!

WANDERERS

The railroad tracks, some mossy shacks,
                A night hawk swooping over;
The industry of droning bee
                In fields of scented clover.
The placid charm of nestled farm,
                Reward of someone's labor;
A vision fleet of housewife neat
                Who chats with friendly neighbor.

As on we go, and on we go
                Not caring where we wander.
We only know that we must know,
                What lies away off yonder.
Let those who plod familiar sod
                Most bitterly deride us,
We little care as on we fare
                With Wanderlust beside us.

A shaded lane, a quiet lane
                That winds through wooded hollow.
A bird's swift thrust from ashen dust
                And dainty notes that follow.
A rainbow bridge from ridge to ridge,
                A rolling peal of thunder.
A brook's soft prayer on summer air,
                That makes us pause in wonder.

So on we go, still on we go,
                Not knowing why we wander.
We only know that we must know,
                What lies away over yonder.
A winding trail, can never fail
                To lead us on, and ever
Will we rejoice to hear the voice
                That whispers on forever.

TO OUR CHILDREN

Your path will never be all roses,
As youthful mind so many times supposes.
It's best to live an unexciting story,
There's so much tinsel in that thing called glory.

And may you have long years of pleasant living,
Which comes with understanding and forgiving.
May you be free of any fear whatever,
Today, tomorrow, and forever.

TIME

Year follows year an endless chase
                That never once curtails,
While we all try to keep the pace,
                By many chosen trails.
Then with surprise we realize,
                And wrinkles verify,
That time is slipping, slipping;
                Swiftly slipping by.

Just yesterday we two were young
                At least that's how it seems;
We knew no care, our songs we sung,
                While weaving fancy schemes.
But then the clock gives us a shock,
                Serves well to notify,
That time is slipping, slipping;
                Swiftly slipping by.

We cannot pick, we cannot choose,
                The hours or the years;
There's no reply if we refuse,
                No notice of our tears.
And on the wall will come the scrawl
                That brooks no alibi,
For time is slipping, slipping;
                Swiftly slipping by.

WHAT WILL MOTHER SAY?

So plain that something was amiss

The way she hung her head.

My carefree, happy little miss

Was blushing fiery red.

Her gaze upon the floor held fast,

And tears not far away;

"I broke a dish," she said at last,

"O, what will Mother say?"

I promised I would take her part,

As we most always do,

And soothed her laden little heart,

With kindest words I knew.

My greatest hope, as time goes on

Is that she'll always weigh,

Her every deed from dawn to dawn,

With, "What will Mother say?"

WHEN COW BELLS PEAL

When on the breath of summertime,

        Comes cow bell pealing faint and low;

They charm as could not temple chime,

        And take me back to long ago.

Down in the fields I used to know,

To saunter in the sun's last glow.

A half-ripe apple clutched in hand,

        The sun fast sailing for the shore;

What fun to roam the pasture land,

        Go looking for the cows once more.

What used to be a dreaded chore

Would hold a thrill unknown before.

How would you like to go with me,

        Down where those cow bells sing refrain,

Imagining the while, that we

        Were youngsters with a world to gain?

Let's tramp the leafy winding lane,

And bring the cows back home again.

THE MAN IN OVERALLS

No matter where you go he's there,
        A most essential part.
And carefully he will prepare
        The groundwork from the start.
Then faithfully he'll follow through
        Until the last lick falls.
We don't pay much attention to
        The man in overalls.

You see him coming from the mines,
        Or straining on a wrench.
You'll find him logging in the pines,
        In rains that chill and drench.
And though sometimes his temper mounts
        At work that gripes and galls,
He gets it done, and that's what counts;
        The man in overalls.

No nation can grow great and strong
        Where workers fudge and shirk;
Each part of it must move along
        By plain old honest work.
Our land stands like a rock today
        So sturdy are its walls.
We never, never can repay
        The man in overalls.

THE PRIZE WINNER

The boys were telling yarns one day,
                A motley crew was there.
The talk was all of windstorms
                To which this earth is heir.

Our champion, well known as Ike
                Said, "Boys listen, while I tell
About a Kansas windstorm
                That could have no parallel.

"This happened many years ago
                When I was just a kid,
A storm came up one summer day,
                And blow, I'll say it did!

"Of course we all went underground,
                Storm cellars give protection,
But we could feel the old earth shake,
                As during an election.

"When we came out the house was gone.
                The barn and henhouse too,
Just like somebody's waved a wand
                The way magicians do.

"While we was all a-standin' there,
                Struck pretty dumb you know,
So help me Hanner, gentlemen,
                We heard our rooster crow.

'Where could he be, the puny fowl?
                All else gone slick and clean.
It didn't even make half sense,
                If you see what I mean.

"We searched around and finally
                We found him all so snug,
His head and neck a-stickin' out
                My father's gallon jug!

"It was the wind that put him there,
                Of that there is no doubt.
The old man had to break his jug
                To get the rooster out!"

We all were used to tallish tales
                So did not criticize.
Instead the boys all voted,
                That Ike should have the prize.

THE WORTHY ONE

I wrote a poem to a maid,

And many were the things I said;

Devotion true, and heart of gold

Used the expressions that are old—

The words have been as often told

        As have man's love for woman.

It seemed to me a work of art

This love song written from the heart;

But Satan-sent there came a doubt

That somehow would not stay without—

Raised ugly head and seemed to shout

        "Wait! Is the lady worthy?"

Another inspiration came,

Upholding inspiration's name;

I did not change the "heart of gold"

Kept all the love expressions old—

I had the sweetest story told

        To dearest one, My Mother.

PAUL BUNYAN'S BOYS

Out in the everlasting hills
              Where mighty trees stand high,
You'll find a crew unknown to frills,
              Outspoken, clear of eye.
Who handle tools of tempered steel
              As children handle toys.
A little checking will reveal
              They are Paul Bunyan's boys.

~~~

The bunkhouse stove was cherry red
              But outside is was cold.
Bill Carey pulled his chair up close
              For he was getting old;
Though maybe he imagined some,
              This is the tale he told.

"Paul Bunyan was a real man
              Not just a made up name.
I worked for him, and so I know
              That he well earned his fame.
For logging to Paul Bunyan, men,
              Was more than just a game.

"Why he was easy twice as strong
              As Atlas at his best.
A brainy man, he coulda passed
              The hardest kind of test;
And you would always find him there
              Where things were liveliest.
Of course he didn't need a crew,
              He was so cussed stout;
He had equipment of the best
              He coulda done without.
He only gave us jobs to do
              To help us people out.

"We got more logs in half a day
                Than most gets in a week.
He'd set in camp ten miles away
                And we could hear him speak;
But if some little thing went wrong
                He'd be there like a streak.

"Don't let some city feller say,
                This history is lies;
Because he wears them horn rim specs
                And thinks that he is wise;
For he can't prove one word ain't so
                No matter how he tries.

"The woods is full of lumberjacks
                A-livin' by his trade,
Who prize the reputation that
                Paul Bunyan went and made;
A reputation that I know
                Can't ever really fade.
"This logging is a kind of life
                That's catching like disease.
Men follow it in the same durned way
                A mouse will follow cheese,
And this is bound to go right on
                As long as there are trees."

~~~

As long as there are logs to haul
                And houses are a need,
Those rugged sons of good old Paul
                Will be there in the lead.
And he who sits before his fire
                In a home that he enjoys,
Owes much for satisfied desire,
                To old Paul Bunyan's boys.

ROOTS

They go blindly reaching, probing
      Searching food so greedily,
Sending life blood to a body,
      That they never, never see.

Slowly probing, slyly grasping,
      For the best that's in the ground;
Theirs a task that must not falter,
      Out of sight and out of sound.

Growing every year, expanding
      With a rare fidelity;
But a part and yet a great one
      In the making of a tree.

CROCUS

Of all nature's wonders arresting the eye,
The most heart clutching sight that I know,
Is the crocus that smiles to a world passing by
While standing knee deep in the snow.

CHILDREN

Tiny the hands but so mighty the pull
            Leading us on where they will.
Taking us into a life that is full
            And ruling the whole domicile.

No living person is ever complete,
            Doesn't quite fit humanity's chart;
Unless childish fingers have robbed all conceit,
            By tugging away at the heart.

Tugging, and tugging, and tugging away,
            Our feelings we cannot define;
We are lucky that strings of the heart do not fray;
            We are lucky who call children "mine."

MY MOTHER

When in due time, I take the bitter cross

That all of us must bear some time or other,

Though friends be unconcerned about my loss.

She will not fail; she never has—my Mother.

TEA KETTLES

Water bubbling in the kettle,
                Steam goes winging on the air,
Glad it has escaped the metal.
                Must have seemed a prison there.

Rising up toward the ceiling,
                Spirals curving 'round and 'round.
Kettles bring a cozy feeling
                For they have a homey sound.

Bubbling, boiling, gently hissing.
                Mighty pleasing to the ear.
Kettles maybe are old fashioned.
                But their song is good to hear.

THE WREN

Your voice isn't much, as you sing in the day,
                Little wren, in your coat of plain brown.
I often have heard, as you twitter away,
                And have watched, as you flit up and down.

I like to sit here, with the window thrown wide,
                All my work for a time laid away,
And hear your voice, filled with a joy you can't hide,
                As you bid your good-bye, to the day.

For then it is steeped with a tender appeal,
                As you sit snuggled down in your nest;
You tell me much plainer than speech could reveal,
                That a happy heart beats in your breast.

When softly comes floating your quaint lullaby,
                Deep within me, a spark warmly glows;
As gently you're bidding a tuneful good-bye,
                To the day, as it draws to a close.

THOSE LITTLE SHOES

Those little shoes upon that chair
        Are patiently awaiting there,
A trusted friend who lies asleep,
        While drowsy night hours softly creep,
And Sandman slyly climbs the stair.

By day they take her everywhere,
        At bedtime hear her whispered prayer,
They with her smile, and with her weep
        Those little shoes.

Though worn and scuffed to her they're fair,
        No other shoes can quite compare.
Tomorrow when the sun will peep
        Through windows, and she wakes from sleep,
Then they will be a happy pair,
        Those little shoes.

WHEN DADDY COMES HOME

When Daddy comes home from the mill little dear,
                He will bounce you about on his knee.
He will tell you the story you so want to hear,
                Of the Brownie who hopped like a flea.
He will sing you the song of the man in the moon,
                Why he always peeps over the hill;
For that noisy old whistle will blow pretty soon,
                And Daddy will come from the mill.

He'll be tired but never too tired we know
                To cuddle his baby a while.
He will toss you about as he rocks to and fro
                For he'll do anything for your smile.
So play with your dolly, have patience and wait
                And the time will soon pass if you will;
We will both go and meet him out there at the gate,
                When Daddy comes home from the mill!

SHAMROCK

You'll find shamrock, if that's what you're seeking,
        Where it always has been from the start.
Nourished with care, it is sure to be there,
        Growing deep in an Irishman's heart.

BEAUTIFUL CHEHALIS

There's a pleasant river valley,
        Lying in a golden haze,
Where the song birds like to dally
        And the anglers go to laze.
From the mountains tall and stately,
        Past long miles of sylvan green,
Flowing on and on sedately
        By the mills of Aberdeen.
What a treasury of beauty
        Hill to green clad hill a-bloom,
Here a hand did master duty;
        Nature's own great living room.
Our descriptive words all fail us,
        Or we'd use them lovingly,
Where the beautiful Chehalis,
        Winds its way down to the sea.

AN ARGUMENT

Two fellows argued, while I listened in;
        They both had reached an age considered wise;
Their subject was the afterlife and sin—
        One, nothing loath to voice a bold surmise.

He was so sure, and so he loudly said,
        "You cannot prove the way this world began!
A man who dies will stay a long time dead,
        For where's your proof, there is a soul in man?"

The other, smiling, said, "Words have no cost,
        Yet arguments at times get out of hand.
If I am wrong, then nothing has been lost—
        If you are wrong, my friend, where do you stand?"

At this, the doubter only hung his head;
        Such argument he'd never faced or known.
I but repeat the words as they were said
        And leave you to reflection all your own.

HOOSIER LAND

I can tell you of the red haws
        Over on persimmon hill,
All about those toothsome paw-paws
        That are growing out there still.
I can tell you of the counties,
        Name you towns—tell where they stand;
Time on end extoll the bounties
        Of that place called Hoosier Land.

I could hold discourse for hours
        Just of watermelons sweet,
There's no equal to the flowers
        And the chestnuts can't be beat.
I can tell you of the spring there,
        How they gather maple sap;
And I've never even been there—
        But I had a Hoosier pap.

For a Hoosier loves to tell you
        Of the place where he was born,
He will do his best to sell you
        On his land of waving corn.
You will read these lines with feeling
        For you'll know each word is true;
Almost get that homesick feeling
        If our pap's a Hoosier too.

HE PLANTED A TREE

It is said for the story has often been told,
That he always looked forward though growing quite old,
That he lived by the rule that each man should expend
Every effort at building, right on to the end.

So he planted a tree in those days long ago,
Out of pure love of beauty, of watching things grow;
Out of greatness of heart that is nature of some,
And for sake of unknown generations to come.

Year by year went its way while the tree branched and grew
Till the vision of one long departed came true,
With a beauty that nature alone can attain
By the help of her servants, the sun and the rain.

Now it whispers a song as it stands by the side
Of the crumbling old mill that he once claimed with pride;
Living proof as it faces the sun at the dawn
That a dreamer may go, yet his dream will live on.

There are many we know who but briefly suppose
That a tree is the simplest of cell life that grows;
But by grace of One who beneficence gives,
That old tree sees and feels as it joyfully lives.

And I firmly believe the old tree understands,
The debt that it owes to those kindly old hands;
I believe it remembers his painstaking care,
And the smile on his face as he planted it there.

IN THE MORNING

When your clock starts in its dinning
        Long before the day is breaking,
And you want to kick it spinning
        To some junk heap in the making.
When you'd like to break your contract
        With the boss and go on snoring;
It is tough to come in contact
        With the cold unwelcome flooring
    In the morning.

If the rain is loudly drumming
        It don't help the feelings any.
Not a time for tuneful humming
        And the gripes are grim and many.
It takes will power of a martyr,
        And the thought of bills come payday;
How you wish that you were smarter,
        Not a common-place employée,
    In the morning.

Wealth and wisdom come with rising
        While the chickens still are snoozing.
But this saying is surprising
        And a little bit confusing.
We would gladly help to gather
        All such simple saws and junk'em;
They just put us in a lather,
        And we're sure they're bosh and buncombe
    In the morning.

IT'S OVER NOW

It's over now, the words are said,
                The swell of taps sad sound,
And rattle of the rifle fire
                That shakes this sacred ground.
His sons and daughters all grown gray,
                With strength that years endow
Conceal their grief and turn away,
                For it is over now.

When very young he staunchly fought
                At Shiloh and Bull Run;
So entered to a man's estate
                With boyhood just begun.
Then marriage and a life of toil,
                Long years behind the plow;
Too busy for one vain regret,
                But that is over now.

And so we see another space
                In ranks now grown so thin,
Still marching in this busy life,
                With faith and discipline.
A valiant ship has gone its way,
                Has sailed with steady prow;
A charted course that leads away,
                For it is over now.

THE SUN TO BED

The old sun has but one great eye,
        Which never closes through the day.
He watches children at their play,
        Then in the evening, says good-bye.

Some say he never rests at all,
        And yet we know he surely must
He is a fellow we can trust,
        And if too tired he would fall.

Perhaps he has a bed up there
        With blankets that are every hue;
There's orange, pink and lots of blue,
        With pillows lying everywhere.

The world keeps going 'round, it's said,
        Just on and on without an end;
But still it's fun if we pretend
        The old sun tucks himself in bed.

SIEGE OF DARKNESS

With our fire built high and roaring,
      Darkness turns a fleeing legion
Lurks in shadow, watches soaring
      Of the flames from safer region
While a cougar from the distance
Lets us know of his existence.

Darkness in the thickets hiding,
      From behind the hemlocks peering;
In and out keeps slipping, gliding,
      Never stops that silent leering.
From the hill a coyote wailing
Just because the moon is failing.

Now for help the fire is calling,
      Slowly feels his vigor waning;
No more fuel to him falling,
      Fizzles, sputters, starts complaining.
Through the night comes softly winging,
Lullaby a fir is singing.

Now the fire is close surrounded,
      Pressing in no longer troubled,
Comes the darkness for he's sounded
      Final charge with strength redoubled.
While a breeze with sadness sighing,
Spreads the news that fire is dying.

Darkness now has won the battle,
      On our blankets he is resting.
From the fire comes a rattle
      With his final breath protesting.
Darkness satisfied with winning
Rules once more, as at the beginning

TALE OF THE DESERT

From somewhere comes a muted steady beat,
      An eerie sound that never seems to fade.
As rhythmic march of men on muffled feet,
      As if by countless ghostly soldiers made.
Out there we hear the ageless sands repeat
The ancient dirge of blasting desert heat.

A desert rover stopped and stood aghast,
      For there beneath the blazing noon day sun,
Was evidence of tragedy long past,
      A grim array of bones-a skeleton.
And as he paused uncertain there before,
A voice arose that shook him to the core.

* * * *

Be on your way! Leave well enough alone,
      For this is but an endless furnace room
Where men are stripped to white and brittle bone,
      As I now am. This is a land of doom.
Here lies the proof, for you can clearly see
What sun and lack of water did for me.

For not a trace of life and joy remain,
      That once was mine long fiery months ago,
When, in another land, I faced the rain
      And felt the soft caress of falling snow.
For when, from voice of Mammon came the call
I took the gamblers' chance—to rise or fall.

I heard a tale of yellow treasure told,
      And as it flew about on every tongue,
Came crazy dreams of claiming tons of gold.
      I sold my farm; *so* from me blindly flung
My heritage, where most face life and smile
And meet old age, contented after while.

I traded all for this, and who can doubt
        That greedy eyes are those, forever blind,
Else why do grasping men seek Hades out
        Without a thought, leave Paradise behind?
I faced this blighted land with fear unknown,
The confidence of fools was all my own.

I traveled mile by mile, spurred on by hope,
        Then had the luck to wake one chilly dawn
To find but piece of broken toggle rope,
        Which meant my stupid burro now was gone.
A fruitless search in palsied haste, and then
I couldn't find my camping place again.

From somewhere came a soft and clammy hand
        That seemed to lightly brush along my spine;
I cursed the beast and every grain of sand
        In voice you'd hardly recognize as mine.
For there with hounding fate, I stood at bay
And saw my cherished plans all swept away.

And so the stage was set—God help a fool!
        Then peering through the cactus rose the torch.
The air that through the night had been so cool,
        Began to dance about, to fry and scorch.
How quickly comes a throat-constricting thirst
When sun and sand unite to do their worst!

Then to my racing mind, a plan at last,
        Those mountains rising there off to the West—
A creek, a river there—was hurried fast
        By strangest fear I ever had possessed.
That frantic urge a rabbit surely feels
When yelping pack is close upon his heels.

Those jagged cliffs are creatures of deceit
        Where wrinkled witches work their ghastly will,
For they began unbroken sly retreat,
        Matched step with step, and frowning hill on hill.
They knew so well the thirst that I must slake,
So kept me slowly trudging in the wake.

My forehead felt the touch of Moloch hand,
        My shirt seemed changed to clinging mustard plaster;
A voice that any child could understand
        Spoke grimly of an hour that meant disaster.
Although my feet felt weighted as with lead
The menace of the dunes drove me ahead.

Once, as I dashed salt water from my eyes
        And looked around, above I saw a speck,
A vulture idly cruising in the skies,
        With keen anticipation, watched my trek.
He circled unconcernedly about,
Too far to hear my wild, inhuman shout.

No water, and my mouth was dry and hot
        As mid-day's breath of parching desert air!
No water, not one cool and shady spot,
        No water in this waste land anywhere!
A beggar never sent his wretched whine
From such a depth of misery as mine.

While that malignant eye gave piercing stare
        From yawning face of pale and bloodless blue,
Those keen edged sword-like rays fell everywhere.
        As bayonets, they ran me thru and thru.
But agony can only grow so strong
And punishment can only last so long.

The mountains vanished now, which meant the door
        Of hope was closed and double-barred to me;
It must have been because my eyes forswore
        Their inborn sense of rugged honesty.
From that bleak hour I had no saving goal;
A compass fails when it has lost the pole.

Fierce longing came to sink away down deep
        In waters of some calm and ice-bound lake,
Where I could soon forget in endless sleep,
        The kind of sleep from which we never wake.
For drowning would be such a pleasant death
Compared to living hell at every breath.

The burning heaps of fiercely clutching sand
        That seem to cry for water—precious water!
The glaring, blinding welter of the sand
        Where everything is crying out for water!
A cactus studded canker on the land,
This desert with its nightmare waste of sand!

Then fancy-crazed, I found a gleaming pool,
        A shining dipper hanging neatly there.
I took long draughts of water, clear and cool,
        And wetted down my singed and tangled hair.
Such fiendish tricks the tortured mind will play
In suffocating heat of desert day.

Then there appeared great beds of dewy flowers,
        Yet no such plants could live and blossom here.
From somewhere came a dear old childhood song,
        With every note a torture to my ear.
Though desolation is a thing complete,
Still I saw flowers and heard that singing sweet.

Then came a call from out across the waste.
        The voice of old acquaintance back at home.
I staggered there in fevered, frantic haste.
        And only saw a grinning. toothless gnome:
A brimming cup! An answer to my prayer,
A cup! It was that thing called prickly pear!

Then after darting lizard things I ran,
        For each, it seemed, had hanging at the back
The only solace known to thirsty man—
        My one desire, a dripping water sack.
But they escaped, those creatures, one and all;
I mouthed a curse on things that live to crawl.

This heat can make the reason peel and crack,
        And so my brain became as dancing flame.
I ripped the clothing from my tortured back—
        A man possessed, a man without a name;
For, faced with odds with which I could not cope,
Long since had vanished reason saving hope.

So many unsuspected things come true,
        So many times our luck is only bad;
A step like mine we never can undo
        By wailing of misfortune we have had.
I simply made a rendezvous with fate—
It happened neither one of us was late.

So, here upon this bleak and lonely dune,
        That aimless futile flight at last was done.
Another victim of man's greatest boon,
        That friend who stoops to treachery, the sun.
Which proves that friends so many times may be
A knotted knout to those like you and me.

Now, as I dream, the dream that is the best
        Is of a stream of rippling icy water.
I often wake with lips in fancy pressed
        To frosted tumbler filled with precious water.
And yet the driest wind that creaks and moans
Is as the dew compared to these white bones!

Go back and tell them what you've heard and seen.
        Go tell them of this grim surprise you've found.
Return to hills that stand in robes of green,
        To where men plant in moist, sweet, swelling ground.
And if you claim to own humanity,
Take one long lingering drink, and think of me.

Beware the fate that always hovers here,
        Beware its ghastly suffocating breath.
It presses in relentlessly, so near
        And lingers in derision after death.
As you can plainly see, as I well know,
Beware, my awe-struck friend! And go! And go!

****

T'he somber voice that told this fateful tale
        Was silenced and the stillness came again.
It merely proves that some are bound to fail;
        That fate has different trails for different men.
That plans we make. though foolish, wise, or just,
So often fall to moulder in the dust.

While still rolls on that muted steady beat,
        That haunting sound that never seems to fade;
As rhythmic march of men on muffled feet,
        As if by countless ghostly soldiers made.
It is the ageless chant the sands repeat,

The ancient dirge of awful desert heat.

THE DAY IS OLD

The day grows old, his eyes now dim
No longer hold that piercing glow;
Benignant calm envelopes him,
His voice is smoother now, and low;
A deeper beauty in his smile;
He has no dread of after while.

He once was eagle eyed and tall,
His shout came loud—"Wake up! I'm here!"
In many ways he sent his call
Vibrating with a jaunty cheer,
"To Work, and do your best by me!
Come! Give me a place in history!"

"We days have price, and I am glad,
That countless thousands cheered my birth;
More precious gifts man never had
That I fling broad-cast to the earth.
I'll warm your blood without the wine
As long as breath of life is mine!"

Well pleased at pleasure he has sent,
This gray and kindly patriarch
Awaits with smile of deep content,
The mighty army of the dark.
He's fading fast—deep shadows play;
Enjoy his presence, while we may!

ON TO OREGON

They bid their pleasant homes good-bye
For a newer land, a western sky,
This band whose deathless battle cry
        Was, "On to Oregon!"

They faced the wide and tricky plain,
The mountain snows, the flooding rain,
They had a goal they would attain
        In distant Oregon.

The oxen plodded day by day,
A seasoned scout made known the way
With gestures that could only say,
        "That way, lies Oregon."

Though danger lurked on every hand,
The swollen stream, an Indian band,
Small obstacles, with promised land
        Afar, in Oregon.

They won the fight, as man will win
When great ambition lives within;
For them a new day would begin
        Out here in Oregon.

They reach their goal and built anew,
By will to work, a dream came true,
Brave men and loyal women too,
        They won our Oregon.

Through ages past a battle call
Has made men dare to rise or fall,
By far, the grandest one of all
        Was on to Oregon.

MANY A TIME

There once was a day when I sat on his knee
        Where I would so gratefully climb.
While he told such wonderful stories to me,
        Yes, many and many a time.

A brave knight errant and his little esquire
        With horses and trappings the best,
As we sat at home by the cheery hearth fire-
        We wandered all over the west.

Our fire was blazing far back on a hill
        And the Indians were lurking about.
And you can be sure that we kept very still
        As we listened for hair raising shout.

We journeyed in lands seldom haunted by man,
        Safely garbed in explorers' array;
We waded swift streams plying prospector's pan
        In the heat of a Mexican day.

We like to look back on the days that we knew,
        Weave a halo about them sublime;
So I've dreamed at my work while the golden hours flew,
        Yes, many and many a time!

LECTURE NUMBER ONE

If you're eight-five or twenty,

Though you skimp or live in plenty,

Here's a thought that's always true past all denying;

Might as well take up the notion

To go drying up the ocean

As to think you'll ever get some place by lying.

'Stead of fibbing just keep quiet

And you'll do much better by it,

You can give the truth a chance without half trying.

Bottle up that nifty whopper

With a good old fashioned stopper,

For you never can get any place by lying.

WISDOM

Before you call the world a cruel name,

        Just stop and think about it just a minute;

Our good old earth is not deserving blame,

        It's just some of the people in it.

A BACHELOR'S SOLILOQUY

Settin' by the fire,
                Punchin' up the blaze,
Makin' it burn higher
                These is chilly days.

Settin' and a-thinkin';
                A bachelor I be,
But bachin' ain't appealin'
                Like it used to be.

Nice to boss the kitchen,
                No one else about,
No one jist a-itchin'
                To up and chase yuh out.

Makes yuh feel like whoopin'
                When yore soul's yore own,
Still I get to droopin'
                All the time alone.

Goin' across the medder
                Tomorry jist to see
If Sary Jones, the widder,
                Feels the same as me.

I could watch the fire,
                She could cook the stew;
My spirit would be higher,
                Maybe her'n would too.

TOOLS

The soldier has a gun, lad,
                He blasts at peaceful shores
A diplomat his pen, lad,
                He gives the soldier chores.
For every man with tools, lad
                Finds happiness or woe,
Let's stick, though we're called fools, lad,
                To plow, and rake, and hoe.

The millionaire has cash, lad
                Sometimes but half a soul.
A gambler has his dice, lad,
                Which he can deftly roll.
We always may stay poor lad,
                But just the same we'll know,
That ours are honest tools, lad,
                The plow, and rake, and hoe.

I love my country well, lad,
                And worship at her shrine,
And what is good for her, lad,
                Is good for me and mine.
And we can serve her best, lad,
                As humble way we go,
With tools we know so well, lad,
                The plow, and rake, and hoe.

WESTPORT

    Out in the night
    A finger light
Points vainly out to sea.
    The fog horn growls
    And hoots and howls
    A hoarse refrain from heavy jowls
Goes booming out to sea.

    When daylight breaks
    The finger shakes
No longer points to sea.
    But down the dawn
    The horn goes on,
    It wails and flails and beats upon
The blanket on the sea.

    When seamen hear
    Their worries clear,
They keep to safer sea.
    While o'er and o'er
    That bellowed roar
    Goes rolling up and down the shore
From watch dog by the sea.

YOUTH AND I

We heard the merry voice of spring,
        It set the world aglow;
We felt that we knew everything
        That there was need to know.
Unfettered was our swift desire,
        And loud the call of fun;
We reckoned but the warmth of fire,
        When youth and I were one.

We did not pause at any chance,
        Nor did we seek the cost;
No time for but a passing glance
        At bridges to be crossed.
As day came swift on teeming day,
        And sun pressed hard on sun,
We threw some worthwhile things away
        When youth and I were one.

It's only human to look back,
        And helpful now and then;
Survey the changeless fading track
        And so march on again.
Though winter lifts his ageing head
        And will not be done,
There's no regret that time has fled
        Since youth and I were one.

A BED TIME TALE

Now sit right here upon my knee
              And listen real quiet,
This good man loved humanity
              And no one can deny it.

I met him when I joined the flag
              Just Honest Abe we called him,
And sonny, I'm not one to brag
              But every soldier loved him.

There wasn't one in our command,
              But quick as you're a-winkin'!
Would jump right up and fight the man
              Who sneered at Abr'am Lincoln.

He was so common and so plain
              Just like we boys a-fightin'.
Though few of us could spell our names
              We wasn't much at writin'.

Yet tears stood in his eyes for us
              When one of us lay bleedin'
And that good man, he prayed for us
              When prayers we was a-needin'.

Yes, Abe, he prayed for everyone,
              When all the land lay bleedin';
And here's a man who thinks, for one,
              More men like him we're needin'.

More men who deal the honest way
            Who meet their fellows squarely,
Who do the best they can each day
            To treat the whole world fairly.

Men never lookin' for a fight,
            To keep the peace, hard tryin'.
Except when some oppose the right,
            Then go in, fists a-flyin'.

Like him, as soon to shake my hand
            As any man's a-livin',
And with that handclasp understand,
            The whole heart would be givin'.

His rules should be engraved in stone
            So every man could read them.
We never get so fully grown
            But what it pays to heed them.

Gave good for good and good for bad,
            His best in fullest measure,
His mem'ry down the years, my lad,
            Has been my greatest treasure.

So, sonny, when you say your prayer,
            And blessin's you're a-thinkin'.
Just ask our God, away up there,
            To be like Abr'am Lincoln.

DROUGHT

The heat recoils from the callous rocks,
        In rippling waves that dance on roof and wall;
At every living thing it fiercely mocks,
        Though they in anguish send a frantic call.

Each sturdy tree in lethargy now stands,
        While drooping leaves hang lifeless on the bough;
Slim twigs as nerveless paralytic hands
        Benumbed by sun, no benefactor now.

The earth hugs grasses tighter to her breast
        And begs for shade to send its scant relief.
Slim thirsting roots probe deep in hopeless quest
        Each passing hour sees approaching grief.

A thousand voices send a fervent prayer,
        A cry of woe, heart breaking in its pain;
It rises on the suffocating air,
        "Send us the rain, the rain!"

DREAMS

Our dreams may be idle as idle can be
    Not a chance they will ever come true;
Of places or things that we never will see
    Or some will-o-the-wisp we pursue.
Though of feathery figments built up by the mind,
    That a breeze would make quiver and fall;
The hour that brings them is never unkind,
    They are still mighty sweet after all.

What treasures they are, though we know they won't last
    We have seen them knocked flying before.
Like when ship swiftly skimming the ocean full mast
    Strikes a rock in full view of the shore.
Our hope corresponds with our will to pretend
    That all good things are close within call;
So we live each one through from beginning to end,
    They are made of pure gold after all.

GOLDEN WEDDING ANNIVERSARY

Fifty long years they've been married,
        Fifty long years to a day,
Worries and troubles they've carried
        Beat them, and chucked them away.

Just like a rock of the ages
        Welded together to last.
Turn back the well written pages,
        Theirs is an envious past.

No room for subtle deceiving,
        Burning so constant the flame
This is the meaning of cleaving,
        Putting so many to shame.

Theirs is no passing emotion,
        Such as we so often find,
Theirs is no doubtful devotion;
        Theirs is the permanent kind.

WHEN DROPS THE VEIL

When those we love, at crossroads take the trail
That leads across to far and unknown land;
When drops that soft impenetrable veil
We face the void, and do not understand.
And as we contemplate the depths of things
We must confess an ignorance sublime;
Though we may question, but the echo rings,
The answer lies in some dim hall of time.

Do those now waiting there observe us here,
And pity us as futile shift we make?
Do those who loved us match us tear for tear
When we high hopes, exalted dreams forsake?
Or does the veil which hides them from our sight
Screen us from them, with same dark robe of night?

CHILD EXPERTS

Those souls who never had a child
                Can never, never, praise them;
Instead they'll calmly set you wild
                By telling how to raise them.

Brave formula that no one knows
                Who has a brood of many;
Why does this knowledge just unclose
                To those who haven't any?

SEALED LIPS

When he returned he used to sit
        And puff a moody cigarette;
Our questions fazed him not one bit,
        He kept his silence, keeps it yet.
There are some things men cannot tell,
And after all, it's just as well.

In Flanders' mud he spent long weeks,
        And in the Argonne so they say,
When, "Tell us, Frank!" somebody speaks,
        He only stares and looks away.
For he has seen in man revealed,
The prowling beast, his lips are sealed.

THE SCOUT

He had to have a cunning agile brain
        And eyes to see what really wasn't there.
He had to know the hills, the endless plain,
        As many of us know our easy chair.

And he could read a trail as we read text,
        Apply the wisdom gained in days long past,
He never knew just what might happen next.
        The first mistake might also be the last.

His independence was a thing apart;
        Fierce his dislike for doors, and locks, and bars.
The open spaces claimed his rugged heart,
        His tent the sky above, his light the stars.

He showed the pioneers the better way;
        Far to the van he always led the rest.
This man to whom we owe the most today,
        The fur-clad scout who led our fathers West.

SURE IT'S SINGING

There are many things that please us,
Shake the blues and make them leave us,
Make us want to tune our pipes and try to sing.
But the song that sets me humming,
Brings the word the summer's coming,
Is the song the frogs give voice to in the spring.

It is hard to catch the measure,
But it brings a real pleasure,
Calls up thoughts of sweetpeas blooming in a row.
Some will say these words are joking,
That a frog is merely croaking,
They just miss the perfect bass, the tremolo.

Frog songs bring a happy feeling,
Make poetic thoughts come stealing,
That a lot of noisy croaking could not do.
Big and little, all together,
Rain or sunshine, any weather,
Here is one who wouldn't stop them; now would you?

TREE PLANTERS

For many years this land was treeless waste,
            The loggers and their engines stripped it clean.
Now those old careless ways have been replaced
            By men who choose to work with evergreen.

By thousands they are growing once again,
            And no one ever sees them but agrees,
No work by any other group of men
            Can quite compare with all these living trees.

Tree planters are but artists, one and all,
            For on this chosen land has been unveiled,
A picture such as never graced a hall,
            And proof to all, that foresight has prevailed.

We gladly lose what was a real fear,
            For here is stocked a lasting treasure chest,
That will grow richer, year on added year;
            We see a new day dawning for our west.

To dream, to map a course, and then to act,
            There is no greater work for any man,
Each step determined fact on proven fact;
            Thank heaven for the kind of men who plan.

SCOTTY

I have known him for years; he's a stranger to fame,
Just a hard working fellow, plain Scotty's his name.
And I knew his wife too—now she took sick and died,
And though he didn't tell me, I knew down inside.
That something was gone he could never replace,
Though not the least sign of it showed in his face.
Just a droop to the shoulders, he couldn't quite hide,
Betraying the fight he was making inside.
But he still wore his smile as he went on alone,
Just the same kind old Scotty, we always had known.

And his wasn't heroics of pasty faced clown,
Who laughs when his structure is clattering down.
Who laughs just because a cheap show must go on
When heart isn't in it and courage is gone.
Old Scotty has grit—purest courage to spare,
And that kind of people don't bow to despair.
For they have what is known as unquenchable spark
Which means they can live on, and smile—in the dark.

So onward he goes, at his work day by day,
A wave and a greeting for children at play;
A handshake that's firm and an eye that don't flinch,
And a sly way of helping a friend through a pinch.
Though you may think it strange that I eulogize so,
Singing praises of one whom so few people know;
This is why: his are traits that we all know as good,
And he speaks and he acts as we know a man should.
It is plain that he marches far out in the van,
In the army of life. Good old Scotty—a man!

RED MURPHY

Red Murphy was a faller in a high grade cutting crew,
        And though he hadn't been long at the work,
He sawed and chopped an expert way, but mastered by a few,
        And he was known as one who would not shirk.

But Red had other notions too outside of falling trees,
        For music was his beacon light in life.
He had a silver trumpet and he loved those shining keys,
        The way a loyal husband loves his wife.

There was a vacant cabin out a half a mile or so;
        A logger will not stand what spoils his rest.
And after supper every night he'd take his horn and go
        Out there alone and play like one possessed.

At night in camp when all was still, faint music drifted by;
        A child could tell that he was getting good.
So now and then some of the boys would listen on the sly,
        The way a group of bashful schoolboys would.

They'd sit outside on handy stumps and hear him trill and glide,
        And never letting on that they were there.
While young Red played song after song they felt a real pride;
        They wished him all the luck and some to spare.

He'd take them back to other days by playing Old Black Joe,
        Then swing upon a catchy dance-time tune.
They figured him a master only in the embryo,
        As they would sit and listen with the moon.

He had a way of playing that was purely all his own,
        And every phrase held all he had to give.
He treated them to melody that they had never known,
        The kind that creeps inside a man to live.

Came softly Annie Laurie while they'd scarcely breathe to hear,
        The Holy City, bringing some regret.
The dark can cover many things, for instance like a tear,
        Just as the mind conceals what we'd forget.

He always ended with one song; it must have been his choice,
        As gently as a saint would sing the Psalms.
They say that trumpet seemed to have an almost human voice,
        When playing that grand lullaby, by Brahms.

There is no doubt that Red was born with music in his soul,
        That he was never meant to swing an axe,
Because he kept those youthful eyes forever on his goal,
        Unmindful of that word we call relax.

On week ends he'd go with the boys in proper logger style,
        Their outings sometimes ended up in jail.
Some rough old friend would get the news with reminiscent smile,
        And then go down and proudly furnish bail.

This is but told to show you that Red Murphy was no saint;
        He was a logger's man down to the ground.
We hold no brief for whitewash, or concealing flaws with paint,
        These are the facts, the way the facts are found.

With month on month of practice soon the time was growing nigh
        When Red would leave to try a new career.
So all of them together made a purse with which to buy
        Some gift to give him as a souvenir.

This illustrates the feeling that those fellows had you see,
    Those rough, strong handed men who bow to none.
The bull-buck* said, "If things don't click come back and work for me,
    But I am sure your logging days are done."

On his last day a widow-maker* hit him on the head,
    The luckless lot of many men before.
His partner took one look at him and knew that he was dead,
    The old man with the scythe had made a score.

His friends packed his belongings with a sadness none can doubt,
    And sent them to his folks across the Sound.
They'd rather seen most anyone that Red be carried out,
    For men like him are quicker lost than found.

Now you may have your mind made up and find it hard to change,
    But we are told he sometimes plays again,
No lumberjack in all the camp considers it as strange,
    And loggers are not superstitious men.

But do not call these hardy men all liars by the clock,
    It's better not to speak than to retract;
But Red still plays his trumpet by that camp up on the Sauk,
    And every mother's son will swear it fact.

Quite often in the drowsy night when all the camp is still,
    Some restless logger hears from far away,
A silver trumpet sounding on the breeze from off the hill,
    And he is sure he hears Red Murphy play.

A bull-buck is the cutting crew foreman.
A widow-maker is a loose limb left hanging in a standing tree.

NIGHT WHISTLE

The hosts of darkness walk unshod
> In the air so damp and chill.

While a prowling coyote's brisk roulade
> Comes rolling from the hill.

Now a whistle comes on midnight wings
> With a mood we can't dispel;

For lonely things are the only things
> That whistles ever tell.

A bell can bring a splendid song
> That can please us to the soul;

With the sweetness of the evensong,
> Or a lilting barcarolle.

But a whistle plucks on dusty strings
> Like a dream that's been astray,

For lonely things are the only things
> That whistles ever say.

ON THE OLD, OLD SUBJECT

What can make the youth go mooning,
               Make the old folks laugh and sing;
Send the lovers out a-spooning,
               As the pleasant breath of spring?

Send the children picking flowers,
               On the slopes along the hill;
Sweep aside the speeding hours,
               Send the urge that's never still?

Point the way to sheltered places,
               Lead our restless feet astray;
Show us gnomes and fairy faces,
               In the woodland on the way?

Make us feel there's Someone present,
               Who maintains a guiding hand;
Brings us thoughts forever pleasant,
               We don't try to understand?

Golden thoughts, we all have had them,
               As we see a new world bring
Leaves and flowers—and we all love them,
               Nothing brings them like the spring!

THE GREEDY PIGGY

A little pig started to market.
           The distance was hardly a mile.
A wee crooked trail that he knew very well
That ran by the farm of the kind Mr. Bell,
           And over a rickety stile.

Now this little piggy was hungry,
           So he squeezed under Mr. Bell's gate.
Hurried where turnips were growing so sweet,
Purple topped turnips, such good things to eat,
           And with relish he ate and he ate.

As you're thinking he acted quite piggish,
           As people do once in a while.
His tummy was stuffed but he didn't feel shame
But he couldn't get out the way that he came,
           And he couldn't get over the stile.

But he finally got home empty handed,
           For he never went on to the store.
His mother was angry and put him to bed,
And he was quite sick too his big brother said,
           Now he isn't sent out any more.

So children, when you go to market,
           Hurry home as you always are bid.
Don't stop at the neighbors to chatter and play
Or you may be sorry for many a day.
           Don't act like the little pig did.

THOSE FRESHIE BOYS

He sat there studying his book,
                A Sophomore lad, so wise;
And all at once he turned and looked
                And opened wide his eyes.

"Such noise," he said, and as he looked,
                His eyes grew large as pears.
"Oh!" said the teacher, "don't you know?
                Just Freshmen on the stairs."

"A class of Freshmen?—such noise!
                Why so much laugh and prattle?
I know, but tho they're mostly boys,
                They sound like herds of cattle."

MINUET IN G

The day breaks and the sun comes up,
                And the clock creeps 'round to nine.
You put your arm around her,
                And go strolling down the line.

You surely do despise her,
                Yet you have to treat her so,
And ever must be kind to her,
                It's courtesy, you know!

You took her home the night before,
                And never gave her a look.
Oh, this is not a girl, my boy:
                But a blessed English book!!

THE BUILDER

Hammer and nails are not of her ken
        Only her beak and a rare artistry,
Backward and forward again and again,
        Building her nest in the old apple tree.

Shaping and molding and making it fast;
        Hammock and house, and crib all in one,
Deep in her work while the hours fly past,
        Taking no rest till her work is all done.

Look at the things that she takes in her bill;
        Grasses and mosses and pieces of thread.
Great is her cunning and stubborn her will,
        Marvelous knowledge in that little head.

Quietly working, too busy to sing,
        Silently shaming the busiest bee;
My little neighbor who came with the spring
        Building a nest in the old apple tree.

MY PUPPY

Tiny and fuzzy, he comes at my call
        Eyes that so cunningly shine;
His the ambition to see and hear all,
        That little puppy of mine.

Wobbly and awkward, most all ears and feet,
        Barking so squeaky and shrill;
Cute little rascal despite his conceit,
        Only in sleep is he still.

Making his bed anywhere that he please,
        Lacking in manners and taste.
Just pick him up though, and give him a squeeze,
        He has affection to waste.

Perfectly happy without pedigree,
        Not a blue blood in his line.
Nuisance to most everybody but me,
        That little puppy of mine.

GOOD-NIGHT

Good-night, dear one, good-night.

Just you alone would know,

As in years long past, our love will last,

And live in a golden glow.

May the breeze sing gentle songs to you

Till we meet in the morning light;

My thoughts go deep, as you lie asleep,

Good-night. Good-night. Good-night.

Good-night, dear one, good-night.

The dark will soon be gone:

May you dream the hours of your precious flowers,

You will see them again at dawn.

You have earned a sweet and quiet rest,

While time makes its noiseless flight.

Till the hour when, comes the day again,

Good-night. Good-night. Good-night.

KEEP HOPIN'

You can rid yourself of worry,
  You can paint a dull sky brighter;
Gloom will leave you in a hurry,
  And your load will seem much lighter.
It's not trouble to keep smilin',
  Makes a new world seem to open,
Keeps the good will kettle bilin'—
  If you always keep a hopin'.

It won't leave you then, that feelin'
  That all things will come out rightly;
Frowns won't never come a-stealing'
  And a frown is real unsightly.
You will feel the joy in labor,
  Folks will never catch you mopin',
You will be a better neighbor—
  If you go thru life a-hopin'.

A TRAGEDY *(Apologies to Poe)*

It wasn't so bloomin' long ago,
    That there sat three seats from me
A cute little Soph, whom you may know,
    By the name of Te-he-he.

I was a Soph and she was the same,
    And it's easy enough to see,
Why the watching, waiting teachers came
    And moved her away from me.

Those schoolma'ms must have envied us,
    And they couldn't leave us be;
And that is the reason, as all Sophs know,
    That they moved her away from me.

But neither the teachers in rooms above
    Nor teachers from over the lea,
Can ever decipher the notes that I get
    From my beautiful Te-he-he.

AT HOME TO-NIGHT

All quiet now, and peace
            Is resting here within;
The days endeavors cease,
            And dusky hours begin.
The stars serenely shine
            From out their awful height,
While here, just me and mine—
            It's sweet at home, to-night!

It's sweet at home to-night!
            So sweet I cannot tell;
As mellow glows the light,
            Comes whisper: "all is well!"
The little ones asleep,
            All in the world is right;
All quiet on the deep—
            It's sweet at home, to-night!

It's sweet at home, to-night!
            May others feel the same,
All sorrow put to flight
            And fear but just a name;
May feel that man is blest,
            And ever in His sight,
That one who gives us rest
            Makes life so sweet to-night.

I hope that those unknown
            Who linger far away,
Full share of peace may own,
            With passing of the day
I pray that One Who knows,
            May lead their steps a-right;
May give them sweet repose,
            And dreams of home, to-night.

AWAKEN THE BOY

Awaken the boy in his heart,
            And won in nine-tenths of the fight;
The boy, who of a man is a part,
            Who slumbers, yet ever so light!

Awaken the boy in his heart,
            The fellow of freckles and tan,
Just win him as friend from the start,
            And you've won forever, the man!

THE QUESTION BOX

He put his playthings to one side
            And smiled so trustfully,
His clear brown eyes, with candor wide
            Looked bravely up at me.

"I'm four 'ears old," he proudly said,
            "Dust four 'ears old today";
Then wisely perked his little head
            To catch what I might say.

Deep subjects he had locked in store
            To his perspective dim,
He thought I might unlock the door
            And thus enlighten him.

He no doubt thought all adults wise.
            I did the best I could
Yet ignorance we can't disguise
            As often times we would.

Dear little knowledge seeking son
            With questions manifold;
He made me sound more like the one
            Who was but four years old.

GRANDMA

Her goodness is past all denying
>She is never quick tempered and curt;
A pat on the back when you're trying
>And the most soothing words when you're hurt.

We all are so loyal around her,
>It is something that can't be defined;
Our grandfather knew when he found her,
>That she'd always be thoughtful and kind.

She's just simply tops as a neighbor,
>For such genuine neighbors are rare,
Who wish us the best for our labor,
>And we love those who honestly care.

We welcome those people like Grandma,
>Who can always find time for a chat;
But we never see many like Grandma,
>And the world is the poorer for that.

THE DEEPEST SILENCE

We all have been in shady haunts,
                That give the soul repose,
Where breeze will never stir a leaf,
                So silently it goes;
But for a quiet you can feel,
                So tense it is, and deep,
Just come and visit my house,
                When baby is asleep!

All day I hear her happy laugh,
                Ring out so full of glee,
Her footsteps patter on the floor,
                A sound that's sweet to me;
But what a stillness falls around,
                As evening shadows creep,
When her dear voice is silent,
                And she lies fast asleep!

A sort of haunting quiet comes,
                That somehow seems unreal,
The tender thots that come to me,
                I never could reveal.
The slender tongues of firelight gleam,
                In silence flare and leap,
For fear they wake the baby,
                When she lies fast asleep!

THE TRICKSTER

The West wind roams the valley,
            He's knocking at my door;
But he won't get inside today
            As he did once before.
He scattered all my papers out,
            And looked around for more.

That sly and tricky fellow
            Will beg and promise so
But open up the door a crack
            And see how hard he'll blow.
He'll turn your paper wrong side out
            And wreck your bungalow.

So let him chase the shadows,
            Or with the swallows glide;
Go roaring out among the trees
            Or down some gully slide,
But he is such a joker that
            He must remain outside.

SELL OUT

Nothing in pain that a human may know,
            Goes so deep in its devilish blend;
Nothing can measure the shock of the blow
            To a man who is sold by a friend.

A BROWNIE'S EXPERIENCE

A wise little Brownie once lived all alone,
               In a snug little cottage of plaster and stone.
He worked every day making all kinds of toys,
               For he liked little girls, and he liked little boys.

One evening when weather was hot as could be,
               He made up his mind to sleep under a tree.
So spreading a blanket, in no time at all
               He was sleeping so soundly, all curled in a ball.

As he slept to a beautiful whippoorwill song,
               Things he'd never imagined began to go wrong.
First a wind sprang to life bringing clouds to the sky,
               Then big raindrops came pattering down from on high.

When at last he awoke he was drenched to the skin;
               How he ran for his cottage and let himself in.
He shed his wet clothing as fast as he could,
               And his flannel pajamas, and bed, felt so good.

Boys and girls, if you ever sleep under a tree,
               You'd better take warning and listen to me;
Remember the Brownie, his case makes it plain,
               It isn't so nice if you're caught in the rain.

DAVY JONES

Old Davy Jones leaned back and roared,
                And snapped his massive knuckles;
"Now hear my words, you won't be bored,
                And pardon me my chuckles.
I've every kind you want to name,
                From minister to mocker,
They missed a play, and lost the game,
                Now they are in my locker.

"My vaults have everything you call
                Of wealth back through the ages.
Whole fleets of ships, and after all
                Just read your written pages.
I have some junks and clippers too,
                I've ancient Phoenician;
My art collection runs from new,
                Back past the ancient Grecian.

"Old Neptune never interferes
                In fact he helps me fully;
He rages like a child in tears
                And cuts up like a bully.
But when he beats some hardy ship,
                Before the crew can dock'er,
I give his royal nibs the slip
                And claim it for my locker."

Old Davy is a stingy man
                He seldom parts with treasure,
Just snatches everything he can,
                And his is all the pleasure.
It never fails that he place
                A curse on all he touches;
Brave seamen run their hardest race
                To keep out of his clutches.

ELMA

We sometimes envy people who have wandered by the Rhone,
                Where smiling skies bloom out in nights of glory.
They are indeed the lucky ones who've kissed the Blarney stone,
                So well remembered is the grand old story,
Some spend their lives in travel like the sons of Romany.
                Ten thousand trails enchant us in the knowing;
But the road that leads to Elma, is the one that calls to me,
                For that is where I'm satisfied with going.

It has given many memories, it's good to recollect,
                The precious gift of love and hearty laughter;
A share of numbing sadness which is what we must expect,
                But sunshine always bound to break through after.
It is having friends and loved ones, wherever they may be,
                That makes us place one spot above another;
And so the road to Elma is the only one for me,
                For it will lead me home, as can no other.

WHAT THE FIR TREE SAID

    The wise old fir tree whispered with a sigh;

    Strange are the ways of men.

    They claim a faith, yet they will lie

    In mire until a storm goes by.

    I face the winds that rant and rave

    And when I fall, there is my grave.

    When once to earth I never rise again.

TO A KITTEN

Although my thoughts were never mean
                I loved you less before,
Than since you climbed high on the screen
                And fell back to the floor.

Be patient kitty, climb with care
                You'll soon be learning how;
You gave us all an awful scare
                You're too ambitious now.

EASILY MISTAKEN

A small boy entered at the door;
>His hair smoothed down by mother's art.
He's for the kindergarten, boys," I said;
>I didn't joke, he looked the part.

To help him out I took the little lad,
>And led him where I thought that he belonged.
Five minutes passed and he returned;
>I plainly saw the youngster had been wronged.

Determined now to help him out, I asked his grade,
>And with Napoleanic tilt of head,
He answered me with words that left me dazed:
>"I am a Freshman, sir," the small boy said.

PROCRASTINATION

This putting things off is a fault it is said
>That can lead us chin-deep into sorrow;
But flying in rages and losing the head,
>Should be always put off till tomorrow.

HALLOW-E'EN

See those goblin faces wander
           In the friendly dark out there;
Hear those footsteps over yonder,
           Roguish laughter on the air.
All outdoors is filled with voices,
           Groups with secret plans convene,
For tonight all youth rejoices
           At the rites of Hallow-e'en.

Small ones wear outlandish faces,
           Some bedecked in queerest taste,
Finding fun in strangest places
           Dashing here and there in haste.
Elders sit inside and listen
           Wondering what some noise may mean.
While above the pale stars glisten
           On the hours of Hallow-e'en.

This the night for youth and spirit,
           Energy that knows no bounds
Dark and damp; they do not fear it
           As they make their waggish rounds
Let us not be too forbidding,
           Not too quick to show our spleen,
Let us take our share of kidding,
           From the youth, on Hallow-e'en.

A WIFE'S MONOLOGUE

Long ago when world was young

                Men dressed in untanned fur.

They talked in harsh and uncouth tongue,

                And not too smart; who said they were?

Their whiskers often reached their knees,

                They only bathed when they fell in;

They saved themselves by climbing trees

                Unmindful how they bruised a shin.

From wilderness to bustling town;

                But men keep manners of the cave.

Now husband lay that paper down!

                Go take a bath! And shave!

WHAT MIND THE RAIN?

What mind the rain, we two?
                Sent by heavens kind;
Rain that was overdue
                Brought by the Western wind.

Must we remain inside,
                Held by an old man's fear?
Shying at drops that glide
                Out of the atmosphere?

Dress you to breast the storm—
                Why cling to quarters mean?
So stifling here, and warm,
                Out there, the air is clean!

What if the heavens frown,
                Hiding the bashful blue?
Raindrops may glisten down—
                What mind the rain, we two?

TOGETHER AGAIN

Brought together, at a party,
        And I heard somebody say,
Neither knew the other coming,
        Else they both had stayed away.

They had quarreled over nothing,
        As so many couples will;
Lived apart, though both unhappy—
        Loving one another still.

Ill at ease, they sat there talking,
        Still too stubborn to forget;
Both had thoughts of years behind them—
        Of the day when they first met.

Then to give their minds diversion,
        Someone brought an album in,
Filled with pictures—some they'd taken
        Long ago, when love crept in.

Once more glowed the flames of romance,
        As they spoke of days of yore,
He with gay abandon kissed her,
        As he often had, before.

They're united now, and happy;
        Miracles will never end.
Brought together by an album
        And the scheming of a friend.

DON'T FORGET YOUR SIRE

He does his best at teaching you,
          So you can stand alone.
His hope goes deep that you're the kind
          A man is proud to own.
No matter what your trouble is
          He'll stand right back of you,
For he keeps a kindly, watchful eye,
          On everything you do.
So try to live a way of life
          You know he will admire;
You'll always stick by mother, lad,
          But don't forget your sire.

He coaches you at chalk line
          As you wait the starting gun;
He's cheering from the side lines
          As the long hard race you run.
He'll wish that he could lend you strength
          As on your way you speed;
He'll cheer to keep your courage up
          In time of greatest need.
So though you're hopelessly outclassed
          Don't cravenly retire,
But hang on, do your level best,
          You owe it to your sire.

SYMPATHY

First I am a senior,
                Second I am a dunce,
Though it isn't complimentary
                To say this all at once.
I'm feeling rather blue today,
                The reason? Can't you see?
My classmates have their credits
                While I have sympathy.

When I was but a freshman
                I labored every day.
Then came examinations
                And I found it didn't pay.
For next day with look of pity
                The teacher said to me—
But say—I won't repeat it
                For it was—sympathy.

I grew to be a sophomore,
                But how I do not know.
Despite my utmost coaxing,
                My grades refused to grow.
Then came examination
                In blessed geometry,
The rest of them got ninety
                While I got—sympathy.

I got to be a junior
                But learn I never could.
I couldn't well expect it, though,
                With a head composed of wood.
My luck refused to aid me,
                My hopes began to flee.
It was the same old story,
                That cursed sympathy.

So now that I'm a senior
                And not to wear a gown,
Why wonder at my raving?
                Why ask me why I frown?
So talk about the weather,
                The trees, the grass, the sea,
But please leave off that record
                The old one—sympathy.

THE LITTLE TYKE

The little tyke who lives next door
Has reached the wise old age of four.
He's active every livelong day,
So serious about his play,
So businesslike with each small chore.

And he has treasures too galore
Such as you've seldom seen before;
        Who salvages things thrown away,
            The little tyke!

He's not a person to ignore,
We listen to his words and more,
        We learn from him to our dismay
        That we have feet of purest clay;
And yet how deeply we adore
            The little tyke!

MEDITATION

Sometimes, when I am at my occupation,
        The gates of thought, a moment drift ajar;
Full mindful of my own most humble station,
        I see how small some big men really are.

We see them have their way without compunction,
        The ceaseless war they wage among themselves;
We see their haughty ways—their silly unction,
        And wonder where they keep their better selves.

And yet the saving grace on this, our planet—
        The balance kept, by more than human brain,
Beyond the power of man to ever plan it;

        The noble heights, some little men attain.

BELL SONG

Hear those mellow church bells ringing,
   What a soothing song they're singing,
What a message they're proclaiming
         As they ring.
   Hear those tones so clear and reaching,
   Calling, calling, and beseeching
Call to those who need reclaiming,
         As they sing.

   Hear the echo, softer, sweeter,
   Still the message of entreater,
Still untroubled, still as stately,
         And as clear.
   May those echoes roll on ever
   May those bells ring on forever;
Ring out slowly and sedately,
         Year by year.

IT CAN'T BE DONE

You may gain the power of Nero,
        Or be a great financial czar,
But you'll never be the hero
        That your young son thinks you are.

SPRING

What can make the youth go mooning,
        Make the old, perk up and sing,
Send the lovers out a-spooning,
        As the gentle voice of spring.

Send the children picking flowers
        In the maples by the hill;
Seem to speed the creeping hours,
        Bring an urge we cannot fill.

Show the way to shady places,
        Lead our feet far, far, astray;
Show us nature's many faces
        In the woodland on the way.

Make us sure there's Someone present
        Who maintains a guiding hand.
Brings us thoughts so deep and pleasant
        We don't try to understand.

May-time thoughts, we all have had them,
        As we see the new year bring
Leaves and flowers, and we all love them,
        Nothing brings them but the spring.

THE BURIAL OF ANSEL TRINE

He lived by no accepted rule,
            All charity was laid aside.
Gave honesty to ridicule,
            And yet owned half the countryside.
The casket with its silent dust
            Cast shadow wholly unbenign;
It seemed that clay brought vague distrust
            To those who'd best known Ansel Trine.

It's sad when one goes on unmissed,
            And yet the fault was his alone.
The miller paid with his own grist,
            The reaper and the crop he'd sown.
The widow long beneath that thumb
            Had copied well his grim design,
Her face almost as cold and numb
            As was the face of Ansel Trine.

Whatever else may come to be,
            Though shifting fate may twist and knot,
Let's hope with earnest fervency
            That few will quite deserve this lot.
A man completely out of tune;
            A man who trampled things divine;
These dark thoughts came that afternoon,
            The day they buried Ansel Trine.

THE VANISHING FOREST

A peaceful legion, swathed in green,
Once camped within this valley lean;
Great bearded fellows, deep of chest
Who, down the years, passed every test
Of winter storm, the only foe
That nature ever let them know.

A singing clan, whose music rang
With purity, the priceless tang
Of earth, and sea, and balsam scent,
Entwined and filled with deep content
And wisdom of the ages past,
In rustic molds of beauty cast.

And each had, written by a pen
Unknown to our most learned men,
A simple yet a binding deed
First written, when the tiny seed
Was planted by the busy wind,
Who works in flight to ease his mind.

As plant by plant raised trusting head,
The wind called clouds who on them shed
A wealth of rain—swept clouds away,
Then pointed out the emerald spray
To August sun, and bade him bless,
And lift a tree to happiness.

And so the trees came to the land
As pioneers, they made their stand.
From virgin soil, they upward grew
Till heads were high toward the blue
Where they could breathe the purest air,
And send their fragrance everywhere.

I heard those forest people play
Their symphonies, announcing day;
I heard that deep-voiced chorus sing
Their lyrics to the coming spring;
I heard them in soft undertone
Speak solemn words to God alone.

At times came liquid notes, as hands
Of waves caressing summer sands,
Or purling sounds, as when the rain
Intones upon the window pane,
A gently rendered lullaby
That leads to drowsiness of eye.

But as the voice of man may change
From low to clear far-reaching range,
So with the trees, yet theirs a scale
That makes the human voice seem frail.
Yet, though the very hills would quake,
No single note would trembling break.

They used to challenge every storm,
Those green clad knights of burly form;
They'd shake their massive limbs and shout
Each to the others, 'round about:
And though they'd weave and creak and bend,
Victorious, emerge at end.

They'd recognize each passing cloud
With lusty shout, and long and loud,
Send cheer on cheer and wave them on,
Till storm died down and wind was gone;
Then whispers came, as tired and spent,
They rested with a staid content.

I used to stand, on winter nights,
And watch them, flooded by the lights
So high above in endless deep
While here and there, one talked in sleep
Or wail, as of a restless child
Came drifting from the shadowed wild.

I saw them wear great coats of snow
With dignity, and row on row;
Then silence was so deep it crept
Into my heart and numbly slept.
When silence walks his chosen hour,
None can escape his gripping power.

That time is past! That day is done!
Now scowling stumps squat in the sun:
And though they're mute and stricken blind,
They seem to brood of years behind
When they were bulwark of a tribe
T'hat words of ours cannot describe.

Destruction looked upon that scene,
Saw there a chance to vent his spleen;
He called his servant versed in art
Of tearing nature's work apart;
Dispatched him quickly to the van,
Then rested; he had faith—in man!

The axes flew, their keen bits sank
Into the wood, and life blood drank;
The keen and cold and hungry saws
Ate living wood with steely jaws;
Then came the lumber jack's loud call.
Which meant another tree would fall.

The strong were taken in their prime,
The young cut down before their time;
The weak, uprooted, torn away,
And ground into the oozy clay.
The donkey engines hissed and roared
While onward, desolation soared.

No living trees were left to seed
That reservoir of builders' need.
They did not leave one single twig,
They did not spare one green leafed sprig.

The flowers which in that forest bloomed
Were at the outset, doubly doomed,
For when fulfilled was last desire,
They gave that wasted land to fire.

Now desolation reigns supreme
Above those stumps—that trash filled stream;
And who but he would care to claim,
A realm we'd hesitate to name?
No one but he would wear a crown
Above a land so beaten down!

The deer have gone, we don't know where,
The prowling coyote whimpers there;
Gay song birds, pausing on their route,
Review wide-eyed, continue mute.
The owl alone sulks there at night
His hollow hoot bemoans the blight.

And those who love the trees that rise
Such dizzy distance to the skies,
Who see such vandalism wrought,
Such peerless beauty brought to naught—
So that great scar, as they pass by,
May well lament, and wonder why.

To cut the trees is well and good.
For all must earn a livelihood;
And yet for twenty years or more
That land has been an open sore
That well we know will never heal
Till men awake and think and feel.

A challenge sharp is written there
That we must face with thoughtful care.
All brought about by heedless brain,
By those who but saw fit to drain
A land of wealth that nature gave,
Then left an open, haunting grave.

A challenge to all thinking men
Who know that we must plant again;
Who look ahead, see future need,
Who would replant with fertile seed
Those blasted acres bare and mean,
Convert that waste once more to green.

Still standing on that distant knoll
Which rises as inverted bowl,
A carefree band rules unafraid,
Though well they know of biting blade;
They sing their songs and, unbowed, wait
The axe and saw, a certain fate.

The monarchs are retreating fast,
Their reign will reach an end at last;
Will childlike men go on until
All black, and silence, lies each hill?
Then wind will sigh to broken stone
and croon a mourning song alone.

COMPANIONS

Beyond that bearded little knoll
          There lives a grave old canyon,
A quiet, solemn, trusting soul,
          Who has as a companion
A laughing river, full of play,
          And though they live together,
They differ as the night and day,
          As June to winter weather.

The little river, filled with pride,
          Sweeps out their mansion daily.
His silent partner moons beside,
          While he is working gaily.
The river swings a ready broom
          With practiced swirling motion,
To clear the leaves out of their room
          He sweeps them to the ocean.

The canyon paints upon the wall
          In green and brown and yellow,
He messes things the worst in fall,
          This quaint and dreamy fellow.
The river never once complains
          Or chides him for his folly,
He swirls and sweeps, yet still remains,
          So full of fun, so jolly.

Year after year these two agree
          In all their household dealing
A visitor will plainly see
          A love there's no concealing.
A union that will never end,
          Dame Nature was the giver;
A canyon and his bosom friend

          A happy little river.

AT GETTYSBURG

At Gettysburg his words were plain,

Yet spoken in prophetic vein;

And those who heard, that day back there,

Stood awed as though at spoken prayer

Of one bowed down by cross of pain.

There are some things we can't explain

So feeble is the human brain,

Yet hope moved in upon despair,

At Gettysburg!

He did not speak those words in vain

For with all mankind they remain,

As proof that he could really share

A peoples' woe, a peoples' care;

He bound the wound, he cleansed the stain,

At Gettysburg!

HUNTERS

Three little men went hunting
           Grave Billie, Pete, and Joe.
Three up and coming fellows,
           Adventure bound, you know.

That night before the hearth fire,
           Joe fibbed of stalking bear.
Told how he shot three times and missed,
           Then chased it to its lair.

Then Billie claimed discovery
           Of richest kind of ore,
A piece of rock he proudly showed,
           Made plans to dig for more.

But Pete just sat there drooping,
           Head nodding as the old.
All he could claim was tired feet,
           A headache and a cold.

THAT WORD GOOD-BYE

A little word but how we fear it,
           It makes us gloomy when we hear it,
We wonder why some always choose it.
           We wish that they would never use it.

CROSSING THE DELAWARE

Menacing ice cakes floated swiftly by,
        Low voiced commands were spoken here and there.
A velvet curtain hid the winter sky,
        Obscuring with its folds, the Delaware.

Grim was the peril lying on before,
        The Hessian army somewhere in the dark;
But not a man who waited on the shore
        Was hesitant when came the word, "embark."

They crossed the stream; with fate walked side by side,
        Well knowing some would feel the reaper's breath.
But men who fight for freedom march with pride
        That has no fear of circumstance or death.

They stormed the enemy and won the fray,
        For men like that can never be outdone;
We must give thanks to them for our today,
        Those loyal men who followed Washington.

LINES ON BURNS

A kindly man once singing at his toil,

Sent from a fresh turned furrow such a note;

A note that held the tang of Ayrshire soil,

And seemed beyond the power of human throat.

In smoky cities people paused to hear,

They with him sang and so were swept along

Into a world that does not have a peer,

And so he captured all who heard his song.

So as we read, and marvel at him now,

At work he did so far above its kind,

We picture his light step behind the plow

While tide of beauty overflowed his mind;

We know that at his birth wealth blessed the door,

No one can say that he was ever poor.

THE DOUBLE CROSS

They have a banner none can justify
            These men who meet no issue face to face;
Past masters with the ready alibi,
            Winning by tricks and think it no disgrace.
They take no gamble such as pitch and toss,
But slyly plan, who serve the double cross.

They do not like a contest with their kind,
            Because of danger that the gun back-fire.
Blood brothers have the little tricks in mind,
            Of cross and double cross for some desire.
They get instead some rash outspoken soul,
And nail his hide around a handy pole.

It takes all kinds of people so they say
            To make a world in which to struggle through;
So maybe they are placed to bring dismay
           On those who like fair play in what they do.
Of all the others, less would be our loss
To banish those who serve the double cross.

TIDE IN, TIDE OUT

The tide was in along the bight,
        At anchor seemed the quay.
Trim fishing boats secured for night,
        Great gulls just in from sea.
The breeze held salty wholesome tang
        As day drew to a close;
While far away a great bell rang.
        What peace! What calm repose!

The tide was out and piling stood
        As skeletons revealed.
Massed barnacles on greenish wood
        No longer were concealed.
No sign of any beauty there,
        There's no romantic spell;
Blue sticky mud is everywhere
        And heavens what a smell!

UNDERSTANDING

We often hear the gray beards say

With sparkling eyes and laughing way,

        "Those were the days!"

All those who mock that aging band,

On second thought would understand.

The old man has his tales to tell,

Has lived them through, so knows them well.

        His words are true.

Those days are breath of life to him,

Those mem'ries never can grow dim.

Long live the oldster and his tales,

Blest be the heart that never fails

        To hear him through.

We all have faults; let everyone

Pray ridicule is never one.

WE CAN! WE WILL! WE MUST!

If we can't have the faith it takes
        To stick by another,
Can't profit by our past mistakes
        Meet brother as a brother;
If we can't have the brain to see
        And heed the warning drums,
Then we are drifting helplessly,
        And we must take what comes.

If we can't lend a helping hand
        Forgetting fatal greed,
And make all others understand
        That good is still our creed;
If we can't hold a guiding light
        That hopeless ones will trust;
We cannot fight a winning fight,
        But we can! We will! We must!

MY OLD HOME TOWN

There are no buildings in my town
With cages running up and down;
No signs in varicolored lights,
Or street cars roaring out o' nights.
      But we have here, nice shady trees,
      Have countless flowers that tempt the bees,
      There blows the cleanest, sweetest breeze.
         In my home town!

And not one millionaire we claim,
No personage, of august fame.
Our park is just a simple place,
No statues stand in silent grace.
      But true friends here, I never lack,
      Who gladly slap me on the back,
      And say: "Come in, Bill, have a snack!"
         In my home town!

Here, long and happy years I've spent,
Each with it's share of deep content;
For as times' robes around us fall,
That's what we seek most after all.
      Tho bragging seems to be my tone,
      I only stand up for my own,
      The finest place I've ever known—
         My old home town!

HOMESICKNESS

If you wish old friends were nearer,
            Long to chat with them once more,
If a certain girl seems dearer
            Than she ever did before;
If above the road and rattle
            Comes a clear and lonely call
You will fight a losing battle
            For you're homesick, lad, that's all.

If the world don't seem as cheery
            As your dreams made it appear,
And you've grown a little weary
            With a work-a-day career;
If an old song sets you sighing
            Till a tear will surely fall,
Then there is no use denying,
            You are homesick, lass, that's all.

THE POETRY OF

Rex B. Valentine

Dedication

Rex B. Valentine

This book is a compilation of the finest collections of poetry of "Two Poets" who were raised from pioneer stock on primitive farms in Grays Harbor County, Washington. Each poet wishes to tell his stories so that the early history of this beautiful area is never lost. Therefore, these original poems are dedicated to all peoples of this area and to everyone who wishes to experience the happenings and spirit of rural life in early Western Washington.

Aknowledgments

The Boling family and other relatives of Elma, Washington has given much help in reviving the excellent poetry of Vandaver Boling, Jr. Eileen Boling, the wife of Van's son Kenneth, has given first –hand information to me of Van's life. Randy Beerbower, a distant relative has been instrumental in recovering pictures and other important information about Van Boling to make this publication possible. He alone has had the necessary details and has gone the extra mile to help me put together an interesting presentation. Having in my possession the 1919 and the 1920 year books of Elma High School has also added to the information of Van's writings, as he was prolific at that time in both stories and poems. Also, the dedicated work of Jami Whisenhunt in helping with the books layout has been appreciated.

Rex B. Valentine

Class Valedictorian of 1952

Rex, age 15, practices shooting hoops against the garage at the farm.

Rex, at the age of 12 proudly standing outside the farm house.

Rex Valentine, at the age of 8 years old, standing beside the family dog, Bob Dog and his brother Randy with their cat Snowball. They're outside their home located up the Wynooche at the end of Wheeler Road.

At 16 years old, Rex caught this steer at the Grays Harbor Fair Calf Scramble. He sold it the next year at a weight of 1025 lbs.

This family photo, taken in 1945 includes Rex's parents, Dorothy and Crosby Valentine, as well as siblings (left to right) Rex, Mark and Randy.

This picture, taken in 2014, shows how Rex still does some work on the farm. Whether it be feeding cattle, raking hay.

REX B. VALENTINE

Crosby and Dorothy (Easter) Valentine were just getting settled as life-long dairy farmers in the Wynooche Valley when their first son, Rex Baker, was born on February 7, 1934. He was soon joined by brother Randy and eleven years later, Mark completed the family.

"Don't do what you like-like what you do" seemed to be the family motto. The boys learned to do their best at whatever they were involved in. Rex excelled at sports and was valedictorian of his high school class. He won a trip to Chicago for his excellent record keeping in 4-H and winning the state dairy judging title. He was active in that organization for 6 years, as a youth and later served as a leader when his own children were involved in 4-H.

For Rex, poetry began with a simple poem he composed at the age of four, and continued with little verses for special occasions. His sophomore English teacher, Mr. John Terry, introduced him to the serious study of Poems, meters, sonnets, narrative style and other accepted practices related to writing good verse. He became hooked and was designated as poet for the school paper and the school annual.

Music also played a big role in his life. As a child he would sing harmony in the evenings with his parents as his mother chorded on the piano while his father played on a Dobro Guitar. In fourth grade he actually organized a boys quartet and worked out the harmonies for each member's part. Band started in the 7th grade. He took up the oboe, playing in the high school orchestra for 6 years but in the marching band played the saxophone. Rex sang in the school chorus and was awarded the Outstanding Musician trophy for his class at graduation. For those years and many thereafter, music compositions occupied his interest but poetry was always there of course, in the form of lyrics. He became a choir director as a young man and developed his voice to become a popular soloist in the community, singing for weddings, funerals and shows. He sang the National Anthem at many of the high school sports events for over 40 years, and on two occasions sang it in the King Dome for the Mariner's baseball games.

He married early and started a career in dairy farming but his plans changed when a back injury forced him to find a less physical way to support his then family of five children namely, Connie, Bart, Bruce, Steve and Marilyn. In 1960 he chose the real estate business to be his new profession. His knowledge of farms and timber coupled with his old drive to achieve propelled him right to the top. His business motto was "Realtor with a Heart."

A side business was produced 1963, which he thoroughly enjoyed, that of dowsing for water. He discovered he could locate water under ground and honed his skill working with well drillers in the area. He successfully dowsed thousands of wells, predicting correct depth and purity of water in 95% of his efforts.

In 1968 a second marriage brought three step children, Kerry, Brady and Tim; three more natural children, Laura, Jenny and Annie; bringing the total to eleven. Real Estate was always the priority, but he kept in the background, a farm and cattle, mostly for the sake of teaching his children a work ethic with Summer haying and Winter feeding which were constant. Church attendance and functions also played a major role in his busy life, always taking his children to Sunday services and special activities.

Once the family began dwindling he started writing seriously, taking classes and learning more about different forms of poetry. He began to chronicle his childhood in narrative poems and stories describing his boyhood adventures and life on the rather primitive farm where they lived. A book entitled "The Rutabaga Patch" was published in 2003 containing a collection of those true story poems including many of his original drawings to illustrate the events he wrote about. A sequel, "Spreading Chestnut Wisdom" followed in 2009 with 60 more drawings. In between came a book, "Tiddlywinks, The Little Horse With Three Ears." It is a big favorite with teachers and young children. "Dowsing Discoveries, Finding Water and Other Mysteries," was also published in 2009, to the pleasure of many readers.

Rex was inducted into the "World Congress of Poets" in 2004 and entered international competitions as well as national. Many of his poems have won awards and are included in his later book "Poetry to Ponder." He was invited to be a guest poet at the 23rd World Congress of Poets Conference in Osaka, Japan in 2014.

Rex felt a definite kinship with Van Boling just reading his beautiful poems, and even more so when studying his life and finding similarities in their life experiences. He believes Van's works are phenomenal examples of excellent poetry, to the extent they rival the best American poets of all time. Rex feels it is a great privilege to share this book and preserve Vandaver Boling's poetic Legacy.

WISDOM

Wisdom has no special season;
nor does it need any style.
Still, if it's enhanced by reason,
will not hurt or foster guile.

Wisdom has a feel for timing,
knowing when to stop or go,
binding ego's bent for climbing,
curbing one's desire to show.

Wisdom loves consideration,
knowing when to get or give,
basking in anticipation
of each person's joy to live.

THE MAN I WANT TO BE

There are those who live their lives as if there was no other.
Their thoughts are only for themselves and seldom for a brother.
They weep with every problem that besets them; what a pity.
To listen to their list of woes would make a person giddy.

At other times with other men, a caring soul emerges
just when one is feeling bad the hurt and pain he purges.

That special soul's appearance may belie his inner grace,
for looks can be deceiving, there's more than form or face.

Compassion, love of fellow man flow from his heart and hands.
Just when one thinks that no one cares, he soothes and understands.

Oh, that I can be like he, who thinks of others first.
That I may living waters give when e'er my brothers thirst.

That I may see with heart and soul as well as with my eyes,
to be aware of others' needs, then help, not criticize.

There is a pattern left for us. It's there for all to see.
I pledge to think of others first and last of all, of me.

PRESERVE BEAUTY

The little pansy poked its pretty face

up through the concrete crevice on the walk.

It's singleness of purpose filled the space,

a tiny crack made for one spindly stalk.

Now why would nature send its beauty queen

to grace a graying path of cement stone,

where careless eyes might miss the lovely scene

and careless feet its royalty dethrone?

The Lord of beauty, love, and elegance,

is not particular where sows his seeds.

A drab and dingy place he might enhance

with lovely flowers 'mid the grisly weeds.

So little purple pansy hold your ground.

May beauty be a beacon to your place,

that all who pass go carefully around

and see the smile upon your pretty face.

RE-RUNS IN THE THEATRE OF LIFE

Birthdays are a special time
when we recount the years.
In looking back we view the film
of happiness and tears.
As images of childhood days
flash quickly through our minds,
like corners of the Big-Little-Books,
or a diary's passionate lines.
Sometimes we may catch a frame
so bold the projector stops.
That picture; so exciting,
oh, so beautiful! It's tops,
until it jogs our memory
of other matchless scenes
including some that never happened
in the real, just dreams.

Sometimes, though, we're brought to tears
by heartaches, failures, pain.
By visions dark, of times we
hope we'll never see again.
Those pictures, stark and sharply
framed with sorrow and despair,
we allow to fade in sunlight, bright;
we cut, we splice, repair.
Forgiveness is that splicing tape,
erasing things of wrong;
healing, patching, with the love
that's part of Heaven's song.
There are those who know that love,
they've shared it all their days.
They've patched their films with love
and goodness in their quiet ways.
They are successes in their fields
as husbands, wives and friends.
Their legacy, their families
on a reel that never ends.

LEARNING TO MILK EVANGELINE

That little baking powder can
I held in my four-year-old hand,
while I squeezed old Evangeline's tit
with the other as I pulled. I wouldn't quit
until the can was nearly full,
and my tiny hand was so tired I couldn't squeeze and pull
anymore. Dad had made for me a little stool
to sit on. Old Evangeline; patient, calm, and cool,
would never lift a foot when I tugged on her
as I learned to milk. The end cow in the line, we were sure
she wouldn't kick or complain no matter how long
I piddled around with her. I could do no wrong.

After a few weeks mother gave me a bigger pail.
It took me longer but, after a while I didn't fail
to fill that five pound lard bucket that sat on the concrete floor.
Soon, it too, became too small. I graduated, therefore,
to a twelve quart galvanized mop-pail. Milking with both hands,
I finally learned to finish her within the time demands.

I was passed five by then. Dad and mom were so pleased.
I had developed my little muscles as I pulled and squeezed.
I found a magic in the rhythm when using both hands,
alternating left and right strokes; milk expands
as it covers the bottom of the bucket.
Sounds of the first squirts into the pail echoed like I had struck it.
When first learning to milk, the streams from the teats
would, many times, miss the little pail, and splat on the concrete.
As I practiced each evening, more and more of the warm sweet milk
ended up in the little bucket. Then foam would develop smooth as silk.

As I grew older and stronger milking became a pleasure.
Brother Randy and I became a help to dad, how much was hard to measure.
We all liked to sing as we were milking together,
harmonizing, and keeping the beat
as we pulled and squeezed each teat.
The milking "chores" were a good example of dad's philosophy.
"Always make your work pleasant by having fun;" a lesson to me.

FIRST THE FIGHT AND THEN THE RIGHT

Some sing the song of a man gone wrong
and say, "Hang down your head, Tom Dooly."
Brother Randy and I with our Daddy did sigh
and say, "You're and orn'ry man, Vic Tooley."

We had a good reason for it was the season
when the cascara bark was a slippin'.
At thirty cents a pound when it was dried and ground
we could forgo the river's skinny dippin'.

We'd rather ride our bikes instead of makin' hikes
cause the Tooley farm was two miles down the road.
We grabbed a gunny sack, told our Daddy we'd be back
with a bag full of bark, a heavy load.

Victor Tooley and his wife had begun their dairy life
by buying the big Louie Neilson farm.
The cows he milked by hand while he farmed the fertile land,
and his wife stayed at the house away from harm.

Across the road from Tooley's house, but in the sight of Tooley's spouse
we deposited our bikes there by the ditch.
We crawled through Tooley's barbed wire fence and crossed his pasture field
from whence
we entered in the land where we'd get rich.
It was Weyerhaeuser property that Dad had rented for a fee,
so we felt safe to peel cascara there.

In time our sack was nearly filled so we set out completely thrilled

with thoughts of silver dollars for each share.

We reached our bikes and tried to find a way that we could latch or bind

the heavy sack to my bicycle rack.

*He growled, I'll take that sack of bark," and when I heard that
gruff remark I clutched the sack as tightly as I could.*

Just then a man burst on the scene, he yelled at us and looked so mean

we cowered from this nameless maniac.

He growled, "I'll take that sack of bark," and when I heard that gruff remark

I clutched the sack as tightly as I could.

"You stole that bark right off my place." "No sir," I said with stricken face.

"We peeled it cross your fence back in the wood."

"Who are you kids; what are your names?" with a big deep voice he did
exclaim.

I swallowed hard then answered, "Valentines."

Though we had never met this man, I knew we had to get a plan

or we would lose our bark to his rapines.

I said, "I want to call my home. May I please use your telephone?

We live just two miles up the road, you know."

I said, "I want to call my home. May I please use your telephone?"

He ripped the sack out of my hands, but then as if he changed his plans,
    Said, "OK, go and use my phone, now go!"
I hurriedly ran in his house, where I could no more hear him grouse,
    and grabbed the hand crank of the telephone.
I rang three "longs" and then three "shorts," I couldn't wait to give reports
    to Mother, she would help us hold our own.
She said, "Hello?" and wondered why I called. Then I began to cry
    as ten year olds will do when things aren't right.
I told my story, begged her come to save us, help us not succumb
    to this mean man who caused us such a fright.
She said, "Your Dad is milking cows, and I can't help you anyhow,
    but Uncle George just came in from Aberdeen.
I'll send him with our pickup truck." "Oh good," I said, "we are in luck,
    'cause Uncle George is also tough and mean."
He was the Dad of Cousin Dick; he got there, we thought, very quick.
    He stopped the truck and threw our cycles in.
He said, "Hey mister, it's not right to take their bark! You wanna fight?

If so, prepare to take it on the chin!!"

But Mr. Tooley backed right down and tossed the sack down on the ground.

Then Uncle George gave him a meaning stare.

While Mr. Tooley looked dumbstruck, George threw the sack into the truck.

We three jumped in and drove away from there.

He said, "Hey mister, it's not right to take their bark! You wanna fight? If so, prepare to take it on the chin!!"

PART II

As time went on we didn't say, "Hi" or wave to him when we went by.

We were afraid of Mr. Tooley's ire.

We hadn't recognized our sin; we crossed his field not asking him,

our trespass lit his temper fuse afire.

He really wasn't all that bad, and looking back it's kinda sad

our first encounter left a sour tone.

One day our Daddy got a call, a frantic one that changed us all

'cause it was Mrs. Tooley on the phone.

"I'm sorry Mister Valentine, but Victor, that good man of mine
is in the hospital in Aberdeen.
He had appendicitis bad; they operated and I'm glad
to know the doctor said there's no gangrene.
But, I hope you'll understand, there's twenty cows to milk by hand
and I have never milked a cow before.
I'm sure it is a mammoth task for you; I really hate to ask,
but could you bring your boys and do his chores?"
Our Dad was quiet for a while, and then he answered with a smile,
"We'll milk our cows first, then we'll come right down."
The double duty had begun and though we tried to make it fun
the eighteen-hour days did cause some frowns.
We little boys did all we could, but I don't know how Dad withstood
the pressure and responsibility.
We'd milk until our arms would ache, then Dad would let us take a break,
but he just seemed to go on endlessly.
Old Victor Tooley soon got well. He'd help us some and we could tell
that he appreciated all we did.
We stayed with it til he grew stronger; we were glad it wasn't longer.
Within two weeks he didn't need us kids.
We never charged him for our aid, but we felt we were still well paid,
for we had helped a neighbor in his need.
He praised us boys from that time on, and we had changed; our anger gone.
It helped us all be friends; yes, friends indeed.

A DOG NAMED BOB

When a farmer is working hard, heavy in debt,
he looks for those shortcuts to help him, and yet,
he must choose them carefully; he must not fail,
especially if it takes milk from his pail.
A dairyman's hours are never enough!
Rising early, late to bed, can be pretty rough.
We Valentine boys had an unusual dad,
tough and dependable, he was ironclad
in his will to succeed at all costs it did seem.
His animals loved him, his dog, cows and team.
When old Rover died, Dad found a "new" dog;
a surprise that it came not from Sears catalog.
His name was just "Bob," so timid he was,
for he had been beaten so hard without cause
by his former owner, he cowered and crawled
if Dad raised his voice anytime that he called
him or pointed his finger at him scoldingly.
Bob was too sensitive and shy, we could see.
It took several months of kindness and love
and romping and playing that he rose above
the fear of a whipping, tongue lashing or worse.
Old Bob had to conquer a crippling curse.
He had a shepherding instinct for cows
and soon brought them in with his muffled bow-wows.
In a black early morn and cows in the field
Dad would send him alone, though the cows were concealed
by the dark, he would start them to come to the barn.
If they didn't hurry he would bark just to warn,
then nip at their heels and chase them a ways.

Then Dad would say, "Easy, Bob," give him some praise,
and send him on back if he missed any strays.
Bob was a "shortcut" that saved Dad much time.
Just saying his name would make the cows mind.
Our farm was divided by the Wynooche River.
The water was cold enough; made us all shiver.
But Bob had long hair, and he loved to swim.
With cows on the other side we would send him
to comb through the brush and chase them across.
They hurried to heed him, for he was their boss.

One day, a farmer who, five miles away,
called up my mother to rudely convey
that some cattle of ours had got in his field
and she better get them out. He wouldn't yield,
he'd call in the law if she didn't come then.
Mother was frantic and told him her plight,
begged him to wait 'til her men came that night,
for Dad was away and we kids were in school,
and she, eight months pregnant, but that orn'ry fool
didn't care. Mom put Bob in the trunk of her car.
When she arrived she thought it bizarre
the man wouldn't help her drive our cattle out.
She let out old Bob and he went round about
and soon had them on the road to our place.
Mother and Bob's five mile cattle chase
was a success. The orn'ry old farmer was known
after that as a cad, a poor neighbor, a drone.
But Bob saved the day, a hero was he

to my mother and dad and my brother and me.

OUR FAIR FEATHERED FRIENDS IN FLIGHT

Feathered flight formations flutter, swoop and glide
in perfect harmonic articulation,
as if to give the birdwatchers who hide,
a show; an aerial presentation.
There must be a leader whose signals they follow,
but how do they know to loop low or soar high?
The starlings, the shore birds, the sparrows, or swallow
all move in sharp chorus each time that they fly.

How fun just to know their flight instructor,
to learn of his secret commands.
They dip left, then right. Where is their conductor?
They take off as one, knowing just how he lands.

Amazing, these birds, who were trained as mere babies,
to take off in perfect formation.
And when they come down there is no time for maybes
their landing creates a sensation.

Sometimes they drop in a tree at its top
as the darkness of evening encroaches.
They each choose a branch, landing with a quick stop,
never stuttering with their approaches.

It seems like we mortals could emulate birds,
in peaceful harmonic endeavors.
Instead of lone acts, we could stampede in herds,
or synchronized flocks without feathers.

But few can abide to adhere to a guide
without trying to change his design.
Especially when his name's classified
and they don't know just who to malign.

So we'll follow along, let the birds sing their song,
and marvel at their coordination.
They'll sweep and they'll swoop and maneuver their group
while we humans express fascination.

HINDSIGHT

It's easier when looking back

to see what might have been,

than springing forward from the pack

to do it now, not then.

LEADERSHIP

Good leadership will never be

a part of what you do

until as follower, you see

the guiding light that's leading you.

PERSISTANCE

Persistence is a virtue when

our goal is worthy of

repeated efforts serving men

and blessed by Father's love.

ROVIN' WITH ROVER

A dog named Rover was their pal, accompanied each trip.
He seldom barked, would never growl, ev'n when his ears they'd grip.
Their farm along the riverside, serene and peaceful home,
was safe, but Mother had denied her little boys could roam.
The river, that exciting draw for boys of two and four,
was sure to beckon, fill with awe and wonder to their core.
One day the oldest disappeared. His mother, frantic, called.
He did not answer, so she feared the river; was appalled
to realize he'd slipped away from her, so careful, she,
who guarded him both night and day and knew where he would be.
Within her mind she pictured him beneath the water cold.
Then running to the river's rim; where was that four year old?
She searched along the riverbank, she peered in placid pools
where he would linger if he sank, where rushing water cools.
While looking up along the trail old Rover came in view.
And holding on to Rover's tail was someone that she knew.
They strolled along so happily as if they had no care.
But Mother acted slappily, she spanked her boy right there.
Yes, her emotions had a race, the joy and then the tear,
to see his darling little face, her boy; the awful fear.
She scolded him for going to the river all alone.
He must go with his mother, who would be his chaperone.
Of course he thought that he was safe with Rover there to guide,
but after that the little waif protected his backside.

Guest Artist

Brady Erickson

Mother acted slappily, she spanked her boy right there!
Yes, her emotions had a race, the joy and then the tear.

SEARCH FOR THE GOLD

There is something good in everything, I find.

Even in the bad, the agency of mind

reverberates the "might have been."

The backboard forgiving the miss

allows an erring effort to succeed. Oh the bliss

of turning sure defeat to victory. The gun

that didn't fire miraculously spawned a new day,

A gift begun

by the crooked bounce of fate,

or by angels in charge

who may deflect the bullets of life or enlarge

the saving shield. In everything good must prevail

if only as a spark to light the next torch. We must not fail

to expect it, desire it, protect it, nurture it,

that something good…opposite of evil, woven

into life's fabrics for us to discover and benefit.

I AM AN AUTHORITY

I am an authority.
I've always been one…
Just looking for a subject
to fit my knowledge.
It's amazing how many specialized
areas don't cry for my expertise.
With all my preparation, and noting
the exceptional amount of ignorance
in the world, you would think
someone, somewhere, would discover
and use my gifts to enhance their endeavors.
But, then, the advertisement of
my abilities is definitely lacking.
Maybe I need an agent.
I tried to hire my wife,
but she didn't cooperate.
She said something about knowing
me too well. Also, she mentioned
that $3.50 an hour did not stimulate
her imagination in my behalf.
Of course, being an authority does have
its drawbacks. Everyone expects so
much of you. Your advice is usually
not heeded even if it's needed.
And if ever required it is more than
likely the middle of the night, or after
their 1st, 2nd, and 3rd choices either
have refused, or are not available.
Then I find it's very difficult to get people
to ask the right questions to match my answers.
Well, at least under the present
circumstances my credentials are seldom
questioned and I never worry about
being wrong because, I am an authority.

THOSE FOOTBALL FEELINGS

There's something about a football game

that doesn't have to do with fame.

Anticipation energizes

every boy whate'er his size is.

If you're a little running back,

or burly lineman on attack,

the thought of every coming game

affects each player's mind the same.

You wonder why the butterflies

cause queasy stomachs in those guys

whose muscles bulge and look so tough,

who hit so hard and play so rough,

but they're just normal down inside

and wonder if they'll play with pride.

The night before a game can be

so long; a sleepless recipe,

a worry time when games are won

or lost before they have begun.

On offense you must catch the ball

and hold on to it when you fall.

The linemen charge and clear the way

and not let up one single play.

You dream and practice through the night

until you get the signals right,

then just before the dawn you sleep

so hard you miss the alarm clock beep.

But when you wake it's with a start!

You've torn the covers all apart

with running, kicking, football dreams

of plays that score, and defense schemes.

You rise and shower, dress and eat,

while in your mind the plays repeat.

Your concentration is not good!

Throughout the day your efforts should

produce much better than they do,

but thoughts of football strangle you.

Somehow the moment does arrive.

Excitement builds, you feel alive.

You don your jersey, pants and pads.

The locker room is full of lads

like you with thoughtful somber faces,

football suits with ties and laces.

When running out upon the field

your aches and pains are quickly healed.

Adrenaline is streaming through

your veins, there's just no stopping you.

That power-pak that you've unleashed

drove out all fear; it's gone! Impeached!

You just can't wait for that first hit.

You exercise and run a bit

until your muscles feel the strain.

If something hurts you don't complain,

you tough it through and hide the limp,

'cause no coach wants to play a gimp.

It's time to start! The Anthem plays.

The flapping flag invades your gaze,

reminding you that through it all,

win or lose, you must stand tall.

And in that moment you feel pride,

a lumpy throat, and warm inside.

The whistle blows, the game begins;

the rising football floats and spins

til it is caught down near the ten.

The speedy runner dodges men

and scampers through til he is creamed!

No scoring here like he had dreamed.

On offense linemen open holes.

On defense they reverse their roles.

Some hits produce a loud report,

reminding us this contact sport

can rattle teeth, or break an arm.

But no one shrinks from certain harm.

The sweat, the pain, desire to win

helps all corral that old pigskin.

The running back squirts through a hole

and crosses his opponent's goal.

A touchdown!! Fans go wild and cheer!!

Why, I can see it all from here.

What great excitement in my breast!

We won the game! My biggest test

was watching while my fist I'd clench;

my part was sitting on the bench.

THE RUTABAGA PATCH

Dad could always make jobs fun,
well, almost always, 'cept for one.
His attitude toward work was cheery,
always positive, not weary.
Still, there was a task we dreaded.
Out behind the barn we headed,
past the big manure pile
down the hill without a smile.
Our sawed off hoes would come in handy
for Dad, myself, and Brother Randy.
The job ahead was easy seen,
rows of rutabagas, green
that stretched forever through the field,
or so it seemed to me, and sealed
a hopeless feeling in my mind,
those rows so long; it was unkind
of Dad to think that we could stay
out in the sun the livelong day
and slowly crawl on hands and knees
to thin the plants and cut the weeds.
Two little boys of six and eight,
it seemed like endless hours to wait
for dinnertime to come at noon.
We didn't sing a happy tune.
In afternoons the sun was hotter,
causing frequent stops for water.
And though it was a lame excuse

the bathroom got extended use.
But Daddy's pace was fast and steady.
We dropped behind, but he was ready
to leave his row and help us out.
His hoe moved swiftly roundabout.
We watched his strokes, it was an art
to see him thin the plants apart,
to leave the right amount of space
between them so they could embrace
the sun and water; grow with vigor.
His rutabagas would be bigger.
Dad seemed happy; didn't mind
the endless hours. He seemed to find
the satisfaction faith can bring—
that age-old sower, reaper thing.
He had the vision of the field
next fall, when all those rows would yield
clean hardy rutes for us to dig;
he saw the plants were very big.
But little boys just couldn't see
the end result, the victory.
We pouted in our misery,
and wished our dad would set us free.
But somehow after days of toil
we finished working in that soil.
In the fall, the wagon drawn
by Tag and Nig began at dawn
to haul the loads of giant rutes.
Our Daddy's plan drew proud salutes,

and we began to realize
our contribution to this prize.
The bin up in the barn was full
enough to feed the cows and bull
for many days to come that fall
with silage, hay, and grain, it all
would keep the milk production high.
Dad would have no feed to buy.
Through cold and wintry days of storm
we milked the cows; our barn was warm
with body heat from cows and calves.
Smells of fodder, dung, and salves
would permeate the stale moist air
and we felt safe and peaceful there.
We sliced those rutes up real thin
when we removed them from the bin.
Dad's big potato-slice machine
worked fine, the slabs were nice and clean.
The old hand crank would sometimes halt;
we'd grab a slice and shake some salt;
those rutabagas were a treat
for any hungry boy to eat.
The stanchioned cows would stretch and strain
to get those rutes mixed with their grain.
By then, we saw in Dad's work plan
|the pleasure shared by cow and man.
Those rutabaga rows were long
but if we'd hoed them with a song
while thinking of the harvest joys

we could have been two happy boys.
The thankfulness that we all share
is--- Daddy made us "hang in there".
That life will never give us gain
without our will to stand some pain.
So if our rows seem long and hard
we'll tough it through and disregard
our thoughts to quit before the end;
we'll follow Daddy's recommend.

The job ahead was easy seen, rows of rutabagas, green, that stretched forever through the field.

WILDFLOWERS AND LOVE

Sonnet #24

A prairie harbors treasures found in spring.
Its see-through grassy dress will come alive
with Nature's own corsage; a lovely thing,
   whose brill'ant colors suddenly arrive.

The yellow Johnny jump-ups set the pace.
The violets and bluebells follow suit.
Wild strawberry's white blossoms fill the space
where later, one can pick its sweet red fruit.

Nostalgically, my grandmother I see,
she's stooping down, her apron spreading wide
enveloping the flowers picked for me.
Her sparkling eyes meet mine with love and pride.

Oh prairie, take me back to long lost joy,
to Grandma's love, and flowers for this boy.

She's stooping down, her apron spreading wide enveloping
the flowers picked for me.

CINDERFELLA

"I want you home by 12:00 o'clock,"
my mother said to me,
"I'll be home, don't worry Mom,"
I said excitedly.
Out the door and to the garage-
our new car was awaiting.
It was a Ford, a '49,
a snappy car for dating.
I was on the football team,
a sophomore at the time.
I hadn't had a lot of dates
but I was in my prime.
In my 16th year,
to drive the car I was at ease.
Beginning at eleven
for a Daddy hard to please,
I learned to drive the tractors, trucks
and car around the farm.
Why, I was kind of proud
that I could drive with just one arm.
When the football game was over
I picked up my girl.
The high school dance was going on,
the kids all in a whirl.
But Betty's parents didn't want
her going to the dance.

If we had gone they would have known;
we couldn't take a chance.
So we just took a little drive,
we ate, we talked, had fun.
The time just seemed to melt away
before it had begun.
Her Father, too, had made it clear
when twelve o'clock had struck
she'd better be inside the house
or she'd be out of luck.
We reached the door five after twelve,
we hadn't watched our clock.

Would you believe the house was dark,
and, yes, the door was locked!

"How will I ever get you in?"
I asked my worried date.
"We dare not wake them up
or they will know that we are late."

"My brother's window opens to the
garage roof," she replied.
"Climb the ladder, scale the roof,
he's sleeping just inside."

Climb the ladder; scale the roof; he's sleeping just inside.

I did as she suggested,
tapping on the window pane.
When he awoke it startled him
he asked me for my name.
I told him who I was and begged him
open the front door.
He obliged; I thanked him for
his brotherly rapport.
But troubles were my lot that night.
While driving to our farm
I seemed to use excessive speed
and noticed with alarm
a car had turned on to our road
behind me quite apace.
What if it were a traffic cop
and he had given chase?

"Oh, no, I'm sure it couldn't be."
I told myself, convinced.
I've never seen one on this road,
I thought, but then I winced;
a feeling filtered over me,
my car was slowing down,
a ticket I could not afford,
my folks would really frown.
My speed was getting slower now,
to 35 did drop.
Just in case the car behind me
did become a cop.
That car did follow closer now,
I slowed to twenty five.
The five miles that we lived from
town became a lengthy drive.
I turned across the Geissler Bridge
as smoothly as I could.
I noticed that my heart was beating
faster than it should.
He followed me! It was a sign
I hoped I wouldn't see.
Just as I drove up to my house
a red light startled me.
We stopped, that red light whirling round,
reflecting on our house.
I knew that penetrating light
my Dad or mom would rouse.

Their bedroom was just 40 feet
from the Patrolman's car.
I could imagine being watched
with Mother's keen radar.
I quickly jumped out from the car
and walked back to the cop.
With wobbly knees and shaking so
I thought that I would drop.
He emerged and greeted me
then cut right to the chase.
"Weren't you going a little fast,
Or were you in a race?"

"I'm going to let you off this time with just a reprimand"

I knew he hadn't clocked me,
but I didn't want to lie.
"I only got to 57,"
was my blunt reply.

"But then I realized my speed-
slowed down to thirty five."
"Let me see your license.
Are you old enough to drive?"
"Oh, yes," I said, and handed him
my license, forced a smile.
He took it, bade me get back
in my car the longest while.
At length he brought it back; a warning
ticket in his hand.
"I'm going to let you off this time
with just a reprimand."
I couldn't wait for him to leave
and douse that darned red light.
I drove the car into the garage
and hid there in the night.
My composure soon returned,
I started out the door.
But somehow slipped and hit the horn,
it gave a blaring roar!
Why is it when our trials come
they pile up on us fast?
There was a chance they didn't wake
until that raucous blast.
Dejectedly I went in to
the washroom of our house.
I stood outside the kitchen door
as quiet as a mouse,

waiting for the kitchen lights
to suddenly come on,
and mother opening the door
to question me til dawn.
But as I waited hope returned,
there was no one in sight.
I slipped my shoes off carefully
and sneaked in by moonlight.
Somehow, though, I banged the kitchen
door as I went by.
Again I stopped expectantly
awaiting an out-cry.
But as I waited quietly
I realized no one stirred.
I softly walked on through the house,
no movement –not a word.
I started up the stairway which
adjoined their bedroom wall.
"I'll slip into my bed," I thought,
'they haven't heard at all."
Then just before I reached the top
a shoe slipped from my grip.
It hit the steps and bounced on down,
a noisy thumping trip.
"Oh no! This time they'll surely wake"
I whispered quietly.
My shoe retrieved, I hurried to
my room dishearten'dly.

But Brother Randy, in his bed,
right along side mine,
was sleeping like a new-born babe,
and had been all the time.
Next morn when getting up at four
to milk the cows with Dad.
I waited for the question-answer
time we sometimes had.
But neither he nor Mom knew
anything about my plight;
so I determined I should not
recall again that night.
Still, after 30 years had passed,
one day I did relate
to them the story never shared.
We laughed at my sad state.
Yes, time takes care of everything;
What seems so big today
may lose importance as we view
it from another way.

A SINNER'S LAMENT

Forgive me, Father, for weaknesses I have not overcome.

Forgive me, Father, for leaving when I could have helped someone.

Forgive me, Father, for resting

when I could have risen to your occasion,

but didn't listen to your gentle persuasion.

Forgive me, Father, for not writing down more of the

beautiful thoughts you caused to grace my mind,

those thoughts of giving, healing, loving, helping,

listening, and being kind.

You have listened to my excuses,

overlooked my abuses,

and forgiven me more than seventy times seven.

You've healed my ills.

It gives me chills

to re-experience the dying and undying

love of your Son to lead me to heaven.

Your sacrifice for me was needed.

If only I had always heeded

your still, small voice as it thundered in my ears.

Forgive me, Father, and help me become

one who acts when he hears.

MILKING THE COWS

Fun in the barn
was what we had,
milking the cows;
Rex, Randy and Dad.

Singing old songs;
harmony rang,
milking a beat to the
songs that we sang.

The sweet smell of hay,
of home grown grey oats,
would waft through the air
and soften our notes.

With Rex milking Speck,
and Randy on Hattie,
we all sang the songs
we learned from our Daddy.

We'll always remember
the fun that we had,
milking the cows,
Rex, Randy and Dad.

Fun in the barn was what we had, milking the cows
—Rex, Randy and Dad.

OPEN DOORS

Nothing much intrigues me more
than coming to an open door.
I'm curious of anything
a newly opened door can bring,
especially if it's a-jar
and I can't see in very far.
I wonder what the circumstance
could be? Coincidental chance
I came along in time to see
that door unlatched and calling me?
Should I step through that open door?
I've never been in there before.
Or should I quell this strong desire
and stop myself, not play with fire?
What is the source that pressures me,
that plays my curiosity?
A wind of ill, or Heaven sent?
What causes this predicament?

I know I've trod this road before.
My soul within, my spirit core
has published truth, directions sure,
to guide with revelation pure.
Decisions I have made before
I ever saw that open door.
So I will reach into my mind;
the answers there I predesigned.
And will not worry anymore.
I'll pass, or take an open door.

PLAN FOR SUCCESS

Sonnet #20

The wise and educated men of old

have given much advice to common man.

Success may come to those in search of gold,

if they who seek devise a perfect plan.

Now, gold is found in many, many forms.

Success to one might be another's lack.

There are no universal plans, or norms,

nor must each road in life be white or black.

However, one should set one's goals high

and spend some time to chart each future course,

expecting, hoping, shooting for the sky,

proceeding forth with faith, and not with force.

One's test is best, when things get out of hand,

but still succeed, though things don't go as planned.

A LESSON OF LIFE

The day was a grey one
with a wintry look.

Two little boys
tired of reading a book,

started to argue,
their boredom to break,

while Mother was pleasantly
baking a cake.

She cautioned them gently
to forego their spat;

but they didn't listen,
each one was a brat,

that day on the farm;
though they rarely did battle

this time they were fighting.
Mom looked for the paddle.

But then a new thought
was crossing her mind.

"You're not nice to me,"
she said. "You are unkind."

"I guess you don't love me,
you're not being good.

I think I'll just leave
and go live in the woods.

She picked up her scarf
tied it over her head,

we couldn't believe she
would do what she said.

She put on her coat
and walked out of the door.

"Come back Mama Dear,"
she heard them implore!

But she kept on walking
they cried as she went,

"There's no place to sleep,
not even a tent."

She kept right on walking,
they followed along.

"We'll be good, Dear Mama,
we know we were wrong.

We promise, we'll
never be ornery again

if you'll just come back."
She turned around then,

and held out her arms,
for a moment time stopped.

Then quickly they ran;
in her bosom they plopped.

"Oh, Mama, dear Mama
there's bears in the trees.

We love you! We love you!
We're sure you would freeze

if you lived in the woods;
you would be lonely, too.

Please don't ever leave us,
we'll be good for you.

Besides, Mama Dear,
we really can't cook!

Who'd wash our soiled clothes;
or read us a book?

Or tape up the wounds
from our whittling knife;

or kiss us, or hug us,
or be Daddy's wife?

She lovingly hugged them,
took each by the hand

and as they walked home
they thought and they planned

how they'd be better boys,
more loving and kind,

and do their chores quickly.
No need to remind

them that quarreling was out
and sharing was in.

They'd trade in a pout
for a big toothy grin.

A lesson was learned
that we couldn't forget.

We needed our Mother
to guide us, and yet,

that wasn't all that
we learned that cold day.

We must live in harmony
at work or at play.

*"Come back, Mama Dear,"
she heard them implore*

HAIRWAYS, OR THE HAIRPECKED HUSBAND

You'd think I was a hair savior
the way she worships me;

as long as I prepare for
hairendous coifery.

She runs hair fingers thusly,
anoints my bushy scalp

with gel that leaves it mussy
until I cry for help!

I feel so hair and mighty
when she achieves "that look"

with hair that's fluffed and flighty
as seen in picthair books.

Yes, I project the powhair
she helps me obtain.

Rapunzel from hair towhair
could nevhair be as vain.

Sometimes I get so weary
I desp'rately resist

the comb and brush, my dearie
wields in hair pretty fist…

to change my look completely,
reshape my crooked head.

But then she sighs so sweetly
when readying for bed,

that I forget my trials
and least of all my hair.

Beautician given styles
are not important there.

I guess it's really worth it,
'til I arise at morn,

the mirror-oh, no, curse it,
looks like a unicorn!

But then, she gives me orders;
"Just wet it down like this,

and fluff it on its borders,"
as she gives me a kiss.

She is my "hair" apparent,
I'll give hair all I can,

at hair command I'll wear it
because I am Hairman.

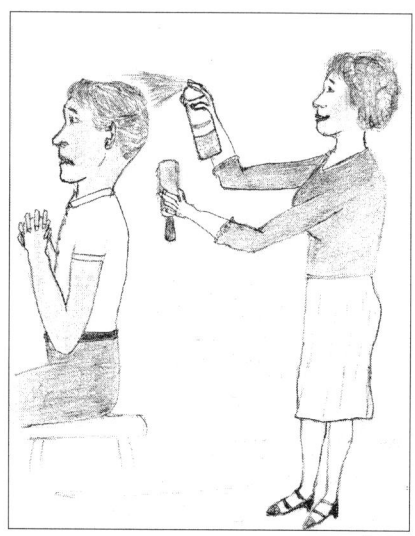

But then, she gives me orders;
"Just wet it down like this,
and fluff it on its borders,"
as she gives me a kiss.

EXPECTATION

Sonnet #17

The grandchild worms his way into your heart,

at first, by chance, evading loving gaze.

Then smiles begin that make you feel a part

of his development, then words, a phrase.

By then you hang on every utterance.

There can't be any other one so smart!

Intelligence just isn't there by chance;

his pedigree says you gave him his start.

And when he learns his ABC's and counts,

you frequently encourage him, repeat,

until his confidence, in time, surmounts

a threshold that is bordering conceit.

What a wonder! He's magnificent, a joy!

He's the best! He's Grandpa's boy.

COUSIN DICK AND THE BEAR

When Cousin Dick came to our farm
Mother was worried we'd suffer from harm.
He led us along those paths untried;
Three little boys, no adventures denied.

One summer day in '42, we set out to explore;
Across the river lay deep woods we'd never seen before.
Randy and I and Cousin Dick started up a stream
that trickled through a canyon small and really made it seem
a pleasant place for us to be and hike that lovely day,
for boys aged 6, 8, and 10; 'twas like a hideaway.

Excitement of the unknown path has made our country great,
and with our fearless leader, Dick, we could emulate
the pioneers from whence we came, who conquered the unknown.
Scouts who blazed the trail ahead feared not to be alone.

Trudging up the small ravine with hills on either side,
I said "what if we see a bear?" and Cousin Dick replied,
"Don't worry, I'd just run him off, I'm not afraid of a bear."
But I was thinking to myself, we would get a scare.

And then we saw, there in the sand, bear tracks along the creek!!
My heart just jumped, those tracks were fresh; I could hardly speak.
In silence now we walked along, slower than before.
"What if we really meet a bear?" I heard myself implore.

Then we saw a nest of bees that he had torn apart.
We glanced around, with wobbly knees, then Randy gave a start;
"I see one!! There, I see his ears!! Up behind that log!"
We looked; his ears went up and down as closer he did jog,
Around the log, we had full view; Wow, what a big old bear'
The biggest one I'd ever seen, by quite a bit, I swear!!

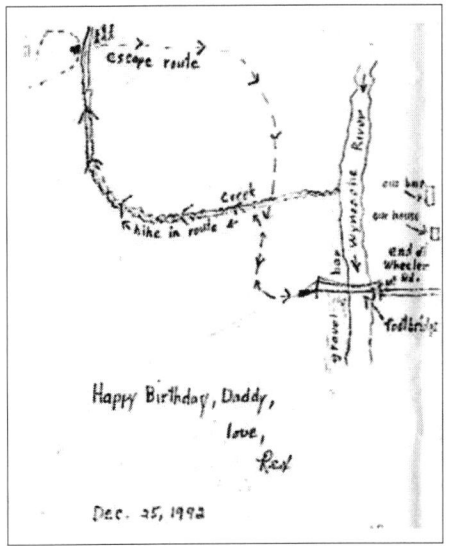

My mind was racing as I saw the trail that he was on
led down a hill to us! I looked for Randy; he was gone;
up in a tree above my head. " He is safe," I said.
And then up a tree I fled; Two branches, both were dead.
I stood upon the highest branch, four feet above the ground.
I would have picked a better tree, but there was none around

I turned to check on Cousin Dick; he hadn't moved at all!
His body frozen in his tracks, I gave a desperate call!
The bear was coming down to him, right beside the stream.
"Get out of there! Dick, Climb a tree!" was my fearful scream.
With one great leap he jumped the creek and sprang up in my tree,
upon that same old rotten limb that barely held up me!
My Daddy said " To scare a bear, you make a lot of noise,"
but when I opened up my mouth I couldn't find my voice.
I finally spoke, a whispered "woof," to scare the bear away.
He cocked his head and looked at me, it seemed, as if to say
"I'm surely not afraid of you," and strolled on up the hill.
And sat beneath a hemlock tree. We kept very still.

Soon he wandered off again, back into the trees.
Two brave explorers, crying now, climbed down with trembling knees.
We called to Randy. "Come on down, Let's get out of here!"
But Randy said " I won't come down, he might come back, I fear"
So Dick and I climbed up the tree and gently pulled him out.
We peeled his clutching hands from limbs that he was wrapped about.
As soon as we got on the ground we struck out through the brush
as fast as we could travel, we were really in a rush.

Of course we went the opposite direction from the bear;
a big detour, way out around; we just got out of there.
We reached the swinging footbridge, stretching o'er the river wide;
Thankfully we strode across and reached the other side.

As we left the footbridge to the safety of our farm,
cousin Dick got brave again, and much to my alarm
he said, "I think I'll get the 22 and shoot that bear."
But we just let the subject drop; we knew he wouldn't dare.

ESCAPE THE HONEY DOOS

Sonnet #23

Retirement is a goal that's on my mind.

Although it hides in crevices of thought,

I dare not let it out, because I find

my wife is planning... and I might get caught.

Right now I know my efforts bring me cash.

If I don't serve my clients it's the worst.

If I retire my schedule will be smashed,

and years of pent-up honey doos come first.

So I've devised a plan that cannot fail.

I'll labor till I'm ninety-one and quit.

I'll grab my wife and hit the travel trail.

We'll sell our place and all the jobs with it.

Then we will cruise and fly the world around,

and settle where no honey doos are found.

WHO WERE THOSE WHO KEPT THE FAITH?

Jesus built His church by those receiving revelation.
Revelation was the Rock; the church's true foundation.
The Saints of God were following the Spirit of the Lord,
that guided them from day to day, His blessings to afford.

Man had learned to follow man while ages dark had ruled;
then God's church returned to earth; by prophets men were schooled.
The persecutors of the Saints, for giving prophets heed,
had burned their homes, their barns, their crops; and left them all in need.

Prophets of the Lord could see a land of beauty fair;
visions of a place of peace for those who'd journey there.
The way was long, the trail so rough, the weather hot or cold.
But Pioneers with faith would go wherever they were told.

Who were those who kept the faith in God and in His leaders?
Who were those who 'round the campfire listened to His readers?
Courageous souls of simple faith who walked or rode or shoved
to reach a place where they could follow Christ, the One they loved.

Wagons rolled and handcarts creaked along through mud and dust.
Weary pilgrims sang their songs of courage and of trust.
The restoration of His gospel strong within their hearts
renewed their energy to drive their wagons, pull their carts.

There were those they left along the trail, those dearest ones.
Some were old, and some were frail; their daughters and their sons,
whose lives were sacrificed to reach the unknown Promised Land.
But faith was strong they'd meet again through God's Eternal Plan.

We, Too, must be pioneers who follow God's commands.
Leaders who will serve our fellow man with helping hands;
with hearts so true and faithful we will never go astray,
no matter what the pressures are, we'll walk the narrow way;

knowing that the sacrifices we'll be asked to make
may be very hard for us—out lives may be at stake.
We hope our strength and courage will be as the pioneers
who listened to the prophets of the Lord in former years.

Who were those who kept the faith? The answer should be clear.
Those of olden times, the martyrs and the pioneers.
and every soul who doesn't deviate from truth and right,
but keeps the faith in Jesus Christ and lives within His light.

AUSTRALIAN HSINKU

The Australian dove into the sea,

afraid of the lightning and thunder.

When he didn't come up, they said,

"Let him be;

he's used to being down under."

FROG HSINKU

The frog fell in the pond.

I could see that he was soaked.

But then he went beyond.

To my surprise, he croaked.

WHY HIS SONG WAS LONG

The trumpet player tooted his song

it went on from night to morn.

The cowboy explained it was the "Cattle Call"

and he was using a real Long-horn.

GOODBYE OLD FRIENDS

A Sonnet

Oh, Wife, dear Wife, you mean so much to me,

your tidiness and cleanliness like gold.

Now, I don't think you mean to be so bold,

but sometimes you go on a dumping spree.

My treasures are not valu'ble to you,

but I don't part with old friends very well.

What if my ten-year oxfords have a smell?

My bowling ball got heavier, it's true.

My jacket and my vest have really shrunk!

Please don't throw them away, I'd miss them so.

And though you think my golf clubs are just junk,

I did go golfing twenty years ago.

I'd better shut my eyes; not see the pile;

and when they're gone-I'll look at you and smile.

MY MIND, A MINE

My mind is a deposit from my Heavenly Creator

with a mother lode of gold in abundance within,

camouflaged by earthy desires and customs.

Infiltrated with passionate thoughts and feelings of "good" and "bad",

so determined by human vehicles of judgment,

my mind expands unevenly with partially filled compartments,

listing first to one side and then another

with the weight of the world and the "wait" of heaven.

I must carefully and constantly mine the gold in its purity

expelling the dross into the slag-piles of hell,

and reject the sludge that builds up,

forming great obstacles that seek to overburden my restless spirit,

angelic impulses, and Christlike desires and directives.

There comes a time when the miner becomes Major,

providing I drop the pick and allow the sluicing waters of Heaven

to wash the impurities from the golden nuggets of my thoughts.

Then, combining my "goldmind" with my soul

I will be instantly transported to the next sphere

in a perfect form when my Creator calls.

GATOR

I got this little pup and called him Gator.
It wasn't long 'til Gator won my heart.
I knew that he would die some day, but later,
while in between we seldom were apart.
Now Gator was a lively, fuzzy pup.
He wiggled happily when I came home;
felt soft against my face when I picked him up;
would seldom leave the house to run and roam.

Now, friends are good, and I have had a few,
but humans often fail the final test.
When times are great they're there, they stick by you,
but when they're tough, they leave with all the rest.
My Gator was a loyal and loving friend.
I talked to him when things were going bad.
When he would lick my face my heart would mend.
He was the kindest chum I ever had.

But now I realize that he has gone.
He'll lick the angels' faces, make them smile.
It's my turn to be true and carry on,
then I will surely see him in a while.

He wiggled happily when I came home;
felt soft against my face when I picked him up.

PRECIOUS WATER

Villanelle #7

Oh, for a drink of water in a glass.
Just water wet and sweet of any brand
from any lake or stream or cool crevasse.

Its value precious, jewels cannot surpass.
When thirst was king; no water was at hand.
Oh, for a drink of water in a glass.

My throat was dry. I'd walked o'er sand and grass,
no water to be had in that dry land
from any lake or stream or cool crevasse.

I staggered 'neath the boiling sun, alas,
mirages fooled me, I could hardly stand.
Oh, for a drink of water in a glass.

I saw a lake so big I could not pass.
But when I reached its shore 'twas rippling sand.
Not any lake or stream or cool crevasse.

Then I awoke! My airplane seat, first class!
The steward said, "I'm here at your command."
"Oh, please, a drink of water in a glass
from any lake or stream or cool crevasse?"

OUR OLD FARMHOUSE SLEEPING PORCH

*We would eat our fill of sweet, juicy, dark cherries,
then slip back into bed with purple stained fingers and lips.*

The big white house looked much smaller now. The front porch with open arms across its entire width still beckoned friend and stranger alike. But thirty years had shrunk the distance between its column posts. The difference explained the equation: boy's eyes minus man's eyes equals shrinkage. As I gazed, visions and feelings of boyhood days tumbled from my memory bag.

Normally we slept in our little attic bedroom, but warm summer nights encouraged a move to our open-air front porch when school was out. We always felt safe and secure on our peaceful Wynooche Valley farm, in or out. The folding bed was unhooked, flattened down, and crawled into, while daylight lingered, by us two little boys. Sheets, blankets and pillows were damp from dewy night air.

Bees, heavy laden with nectar were finishing their last flight before night, crawling up the end column post and disappearing through a hole into the porch attic. Our homemade rubber guns shot sliced rubber inner tube rings stretched tight over their wooden frames by squeezing the clothespin trigger. Some bees didn't make the attic, and when we missed they would "dive bomb" the bed. We hid under the covers 'til the "air raid" was over.

Boys are always hungry. In June, we would quietly slip out of bed in just our shorts. I still can feel the sensation of soft grass under my feet with dewdrops squishing up between my toes as we ran across the lawn to climb the big Bing cherry tree. We would eat our fill of sweet, juicy, dark cherries, then slip back into bed with purple stained fingers and lips.

Night sounds crept upon us as darkness settled in, yodeling meadowlarks had ceased their melodic instruction period at dusk. Big white owls hooted as they hunted. Choruses of croaking frogs sounded like each frog was singing from a different page until their leader's baton fell when danger approached and they all silenced at once. A coyote family would keep track of each other by running up and down the scale with their shrill night-piercing yips. At times a welcome summer rain would spit, sputter and then spatter its refreshing noisy shower on the roof overhead. We kept warm, snug and dry under the covers.

We couldn't stay awake long. Two little boys, very tired from a long active day of work and play, would chat and listen—chat and listen—listen—listen---listen--.

A MIDNIGHT VISITOR

The attic bedroom of our farmhouse was a restive place.
No television, radio, loud noises in our space.
With fifteen miles of country road between our house and town,
our sleep was seldom interrupted after laying down.
No tractors in our neighborhood, some neighbors couldn't drive.
No power mowers for our lawns, no bands played rock or jive.
It was a peaceful place to sleep, for Randy and for me.
But one night we awakened, it was dark; we couldn't see.
Some growling snarling noises underneath our house were heard.
And then our dog was barking with a muffled woofy word.
Things grew quiet after that; we drifted back toward sleep,
until our nostrils caught a drift that almost made us weep.
That pungent smell we knew so well that hurt our eyes and nose,
it seemed to permeate our house and stayed 'til we arose.
Next morn we jumped into our working clothes and went outside.
The stinky smell was all around, from it we couldn't hide.
The skunk had fought old Bob, our dog, beneath our house that night.

We couldn't tell who won or lost, but 'twas a dreadful fight.

Old Bob dog acted rather ill and seemed embarrassed too.

He hung his head as if to say "I did my best for you."

*Old Bob dog acted rather ill and seemed embarrassed too.
He hung his head as if to say, "I did my best for you."*

We milked the cows and did our chores 'til breakfast time arrived.

With Mother's oatmeal mush, crisp bacon, eggs, our strength revived.

We shed our smelly clothes and donned our school clothes from the hook.

We each picked up our homework, paper, pencil and a book

and headed for the road where we could wait to catch the bus.

We had a marble game while waiting, which was fun for us.

The school bus stopped, we climbed aboard, and in our seats did plunk,

when suddenly the kids all yelled, "P.U., you smell like skunk!"

Just like old Bob, we hung our heads, for we were rather shy.

We didn't know just what to do, so we began to cry.

We loved to go to school each day, excited for the chance,

but now with smelly underclothes, and stinky shirt and pants, we quickly hopped back out the door and sadly said, "goodbye."

But Mr. Harner, driver of our bus; a real nice guy,

felt sorry for us little boys and when he saw us cry,

said "Run back home and change your clothes, we'll wait right here for you."

"Gosh, yes, we'll really hurry!" Then into the house we flew.

We ran upstairs, threw off our clothes, dug in our dresser drawer.

Down in the bottom were the clothes we wore the year before.

The shirts and pants were faded now with patches on the knees.

We hoped they didn't smell so bad the kids again would tease.

We quickly put them on and hurried back, got on the bus.

The smell was very faint this time, they didn't make a fuss.

We were a little late for school, but no one said too much.

Mr. Harner smoothed it over so we weren't "in Dutch."

DESSERT FIRST

I prefer to eat dessert first!
Why should I take a chance?
There may not be any left, that's the worst,
and I find there's no recompense.

When it's gone, it's gone,
to be seen no more.
Not even a smell lingers on
like you had before.

Besides, dessert first will help my weight.
No one wants to be skinny.
Then I'll know how much room on my plate
to leave for veggies and fruit, if any.

At a buffet I'm hardly able,
when they push and shove, to be first in line.
So I start at the other end of the table
where the pie and the cake soon are mine.

FIRST AND LAST KISS-
LIGHTNING STRIKES TWICE

It was in the seventh grade a "new girl" had appeared.
Her Daddy bought the shoe-shop over town.
When introduced as Beverly, a part within me cheered,
her hair was dark, her eyes were hazel-brown.

She moved with graceful sturdiness, determined, in a way,
that led me to believe she was a pearl.
She had that certain something; 'twas hard for me to say
what made her that exciting kind of girl.

It wasn't her great beauty that struck that cord in me,
though she a pleasant damsel to observe.
It could have been her intellect, her smile, her purity,
or could have been a full and rounding curve.

She brought a freshness to our gang, an element of class,
was more advanced, she knew more than we did.
And could she play the piano! Classical and jazz;
performances above the average kid.

I thought, to know her better, I'd ask her for a date,
although she'd had a boyfriend for a while.
Her answer was affirmative, my pride did stimulate;
she lavished on me her endearing smile.

*It was a fleeting kiss,
she sighed, and then
two words I heard.*

I'd never had a date before, experience exempt,
but I designed a plan that couldn't miss.
And though I was a neophyte-This was my first attempt,
I practiced how to ask her for a kiss.

My parents, dear, assisted me, they drove me to the show.
The theater was near her father's store.
They lived in back. I guess it was a half a block, or so,
I walked, and bravely knocked upon her door.

She was awaiting breathlessly and bade me come inside.
She introduced me to her Mom and Dad.
I don't remember how they looked, or if they laughed or cried,
but I still see the ruby lips she had.

We took our time; we slowly walked back to the picture show,
sat in the back, I held her pretty hand.
My folks were sitting toward the front, and little did they know
the fun we had. They wouldn't understand.

When it was over we returned and stood at her front door.
The porch was dark, we were alone at last.
My Mom and Dad were waiting in their car for me, therefore,
I had to make my move and make it fast.

I put my arms around her, but before I said a word
I felt her ruby lips as she found mine.
It was a fleeting kiss, she sighed, and then two words I heard.
"Oh Kenny!!" It was not Rex Valentine.

I was glad it shook her so she knew not where she was,
but "Kenny" was her "steady" former beau.
I left and hurried to the car; my pride was hurt because
with all my charm, my name she didn't know.

I decided then and there I wouldn't waste my time.
We stayed good friends until her family moved.
I thought of her quite often, but I wouldn't spend a dime
to look her up-my pride just disapproved.

But then, one day she came again to our beloved class.
She found a boyfriend very soon it seemed.
It was our sophomore year, and behold, It came to pass,
my interest in her gradually redeemed.

I took her home one evening from a doings at the school.
We talked, we laughed, we had a lot of fun.
I had the urge to kiss her, but I thought, "you silly fool,
you better walk away, you better run."

But still, the flame of love arose-to it I did succumb.
I gently kissed her lips and held her tight.
And then I heard two words again, how could I be so dumb?
She sighed, "Oh Leo!!"-Guess it served me right.

Oh well, I tried and failed in my romantic escapades.
But then, I guess I learned a thing or two.
Don't be too anxious, give her time until her old love fades.
Yes, that is what a young lad has to do.

And then I heard two words again, how could I be so dumb?

FROM BELT TO SUSPENDERS

Sonnet #9

My belt size is increasing

as I am growing older.

I'm really not obesing,

just narrowing my shoulders.

But now my pants are dragging;

my belt is at a tilt.

So I have stopped all bragging

about how well I'm built.

I think I'll wear suspenders;

they'll give me peace of mind,

and when I'm doing benders

you won't see my behind.

Does it really matter

if I keep getting fatter?

TOMMY

After fifty seven years, still some lingering pain
clings stubbornly to my wounded heart
like patches of snow separated on a rolling plain,
still resisting the warmth so a final melt can start.

The cold wintry day began early; we helped milk the cows,
did had-to chores, walked our three quarter mile
to catch the school bus while Dad fed chickens and sows.
He put Mother in the '37 Ford 2-door sedan with a smile
of anticipation. She labored hard on the farm to make
our home run smoothly, but this labor would produce
a long awaited child, we all hoped would be a girl for Mom's sake.
Randy and I wanted to go with them, but school allowed no excuse.
We were excited and full of two hopes; that it would snow,
and that the baby would be a girl, Mom's first to be born
in a hospital bed, instead of waiting for the doctor to show.
*(Dr. Lightfoot would have had a 16mile drive up
the Wynooche Valley that morn.)*

The day seemed longer than a January 4th day should be.
It became harder to study as the snow began to softly float
from a darkened sky. When the last bell rang we were free.
We hurriedly ran to our school bus, each donning a warm coat.

The road was slick. Our driver carefully maneuvered the bus
over the winding 25-mile route, stopping at our hilltop.
The road was white. As we walked home, excitement grew within us.
The falling snow filling our first hope now threatened to stop.
But soon we would know if it was a girl (hope number two.)

Daddy was late getting home, the house felt empty and cold.
Without mother there we had more chores to do,
but we did them as we had been told.
When Daddy came into the house the woodstove was going.
we had split the kindling and laid a nice fire.
Out side the snow had stopped, the wind had quit blowing.
We rushed to him, his strong arms encircling us and our desire
to know if the new baby was a sister or a brother.
But then we noticed the sadness and worry in Daddy's face.
We cautiously asked him, "Is it a girl?" and "How is Mother?"
"I think Mama is going to be alright." Then, tightening his embrace,
he added, "But the little baby boy died." Too stunned to cry,
we slowly made our way to the barn to begin milking chores.
The sad silence was occasionally broken with questions of why?
"Why did he die, Daddy?" as we fed the calves and swept the floors.
"I don't know, boys," he said, "but he was perfectly beautiful."
"Can we see him?" we asked hopefully, finishing our work at last.
"We'll go to the hospital tomorrow after chores, you've been very dutiful."

"Mama doesn't know yet. I don't want to tell her.
Morning will be here too fast."

After the morning milking was done we drove down to Aberdeen.
We were anxious to see our Mother, but apprehensive to view little brother.
The hospital corridors seemed hollow, sterile, mysterious, and clean.
Mother was glad to see us, but had been told one excuse after the other
when she asked to see her baby. She said, "I know there's something wrong,
Crosby, what is it? Did I have a girl?" Daddy, noticing she had cried,
took her hands in his and kissed her cheek, trying to appear strong.
With great effort he said, "Mama you had a pretty little boy, but he died."
Mother burst into tears, emitting a low, throaty, anguishing wail.
We boys also began to cry and I'll never forget the feeling I had
of excruciating heartfelt pain when my Daddy's face grew pale
and his body shook with great sobs. This was my Dad,
whom I had never seen cry before; the strength under us all.
We held each other a long time until Mother's cries subsided.
There was really no one left to lean on or anyone to call,
but we shared the same love for each other, steadfast, undivided.

We had never all gone to church together or had family prayer.
We didn't know Jesus Christ, or of His unconditional love,
or of His promise to us, that our burdens He would gladly bear,
or that a loving Heavenly Father sent His angels to us from above.
We didn't know His strength and love that one day we would share.

That the perfect little boy may have been too good to suffer through
the trying years ahead, the world becoming wicked, and life, at times, unfair.
Mother had to blame someone for little Tommy's death.
Who made the miscue?
He got excessive ether in his lungs, the nurses said, but no one knew
he was in trouble. They all were tending to Mother; he was not in view,
and when they checked him he was gone- there was nothing they could do.
Dr. Lightfoot got the blame for letting Tommy die, then she blamed another.
A Mother's love, so fierce and strong-she didn't know God's plan.
He had let her baby die. He hadn't saved our little brother.
She felt punished without a reason. She didn't understand
or know His wisdom, greater far than she could comprehend.

We had a graveside service at the Wynooche Cemetery.
Just Daddy and us boys were there, Mother didn't attend.
We had only seen him once; so hard it was to bury
that little coffin in the ground. It held that tiny boy
whom we all loved but never got to know,
or hear him cry, or laugh, or share the joy
of his first steps and words. We longed to watch him grow
into a playmate, a teen, a man…that little boy…
In looking back, it's like we crammed a lifetime in
that half hour at his grave that nothing could destroy.
And I know God's plan. We will be together again.

It was very hard for Mother to recover and heal.
Her breasts, ready to suckle, became terribly infected.
The loss of the baby was magnified and became very real.
The double pain, physical and mental, was worse than she expected.
After a few months, though, we were told exciting news,
another baby was due to arrive in May of 1945.
Anticipation drove our hopes and thoughts, we were all enthused,
maybe it would be a girl, but for sure it would stay alive.
Mark was born the 9th of May, a bright and beautiful boy.
Mother didn't get her girl but soon forgot to pine,
her precious son did steal her heart; became her greatest joy.
We all loved him dearly. Still, Mother had to resign
herself to, and accept the fact, that she would never have a girl.
Her bitterness toward God for the loss of our little brother
gradually lessened and her grief subsided as Mark filled
the painful void in her life, and encouraged her to be a great Mother,
as she was before that cold January day when a little heart was stilled.

We had only seen him once; so hard it was to bury that coffin in the ground.

WHAT HAPPENED TO THE STUMPS

The stumps were gone, where did they go?
There are but few of us who know
the story of the stumps.
'Twas nothing left, not even lumps.

Except in neighbor Doerge's yard.
A great big piece of wood fell hard
from out the sky without a warning,
a thousand feet away that morning.

Wes Hall came to our farm and said,
"We need to blow two stumps by the shed.
They're only ten feet from the shop,
and near the barn, but that won't stop

us. They must go! We'll drill a hole
beneath each stump. It is our goal
to lift them from the ground real clean,
so they won't clutter up the scene."

Wes Hall, the owner of the farm,
a burley logger with little charm,
had blown a lot of stumps before,
but not alongside window, door,

or any buildings, such as these.
The stumps he "shot" were in the trees
where he could blow them all in two
not worrying which way they flew.

And so we took a two-inch auger,
drilled two holes, just like a logger.
Beneath each two-foot stump we packed
six sticks of dynamite. Wes didn't act

uncertain, seemed to know his trade,
but I was starting to be afraid
we'd blow those buildings all apart,
and that just wouldn't be real smart.

He lit the fuse. While it was burning
toward the stumps, his mind was churning.
He yelled at me, "Too many sticks?"
I nodded; we were in a fix!

He yelled again, "Go in the shed
and get the canvas tarp," he said,
"And throw it on the stumps to slow
the blast!" I did it very fast.

The fuse was almost to the end.
We sprinted to the barn, and then,
just as we slipped behind its shield
and felt that we were quite concealed,

*The fuse was almost to the end.
We sprinted to the barn, and then…*

the charge went off, a mighty blast!
We waited, then peeked out at last.
Smoke was floating all around,
and rocks falling to the ground

The smoke then cleared; we ventured out.
That dynamite sure had a clout.
We looked around to see the stumps,
but they were gone; no little clumps

of wood we found. 'Twas nothing there
but two big holes all filled with air.
The canvas tarp was a mystery,
just one small piece up in a tree

about a hundred yards away.
"We'll buy another one today,"
said Mr. Hall. He was enthused,
no window broke, no building bruised.

Congratulations were in store!
No ugly stumps there anymore.
Why the worry? Why the doubt?
Wes knew how to blow stumps out.

Then from the house, my wife ran out.
"Phone call for you," I heard her shout.
Mrs. Doerge was on the phone.
While sitting in her house alone,

she heard the blast, then heard a thump.
In her front yard she saw a stump.
She marveled that the thing appeared.
In fact, she thought it mighty weird

a stump should fall from out the sky,
and wondered if we might know why?
I said, "A stump fell from the air?
hold on, we'll be right over there."

We jumped into the pickup truck,
and as we drove, spoke of our luck.
That stump was in a flowerbed,
not crashing through their roof instead.

We loaded up the airborne wood.
We said good-bye; as neighbors should.
The stump we dumped out in our brush
away from things that it might crush.

The second stump was never found,
though cautiously we looked around.
It might be where all good ones go,
instead of falling down below.

The stumps were gone; where did they go?
There are but few of us who know
the story of the stumps.
'Twas nothing left, not even lumps,

Except in neighbor Doerge's yard.
A great big piece of wood fell hard
from out the sky without a warning,
a thousand feet away that morning.

THE PARADIGM OF A FENCE

One hundred seventy milk cows eat a lot of hay,
silage, grain, and brewers malt, on a winter's day.
And water by the gallons, they will tank away,
in making natures greatest food; a miracle they say.

Besides the milk that they produce, I'm telling you for sure,
the piles and piles of other stuff is what we call manure.
It's through the winter, cold and wet, that if it accumulates,
we spread it on the pasture ground each time a storm abates.

It was a gray and cloudy day, the rain and floods were gone.
Arising early I had milked the cows before the dawn,
gassed and oiled the tractor, hooked the manure spreader on,
and spread a half -a-dozen loads, each load about a ton.

My partner came out from his house and said, "Let's take a walk."
I had Laurence take my place so we could plan and talk.
We went down the cattle lane with fields on either side,
discussing how we'd work these fields when springtime did abide.

The John Deere tractor went by us and turned in through the gate
where I had hauled the loads before; yes, Laurence drove it straight
into the ruts that I had cut, and yes, he got it stuck.
He was going through too slow for all that mud and muck.

Laurence Baybarz was a man I'd hired, my farming hand.
His slowness sometimes flustered me; was all that I could stand.
For now he had to get a fork; pitch off the load by hand,
then hook our other tractor on, tow it to firmer land.

I told my partner then and there, I'd fill the holes next day.
I'd call up Roger Landberg with his gravel truck and say
"Bring a couple loads and plug the holes in our gateway."
But then my partner, Gordon, asked how much we'd have to pay?

I answered, "Thirty-five a load; he'd get it done by noon."
Gordon walked up to the fence; "I'll fix the thing real soon."
Three posts down from the open gate he snipped the wires in two
with pliers from his pocket, "There, now Laurence can get through."

It may seem like a little thing to cut somebody's fence,
but, really, I was horrified, emotions in suspense.
My Dad had taught me how to make a straight and sturdy line,
that fencing was important, represents a farm's design.

It almost seemed a sacrilege, against a farmer's rules,
I'd built them and repaired them with my special fencing tools.
They seemed to be a symbol, those enclosing posts and wires,
now Gordon Goeres punctured it with one snip of his pliers.

"You cut the fence," I blurted out, "you ruined it you know!"
Then Gordon looked at me and smiled to soften up the blow.
"Just how much time will it take to fix it back next spring?"
"Oh, about ten minutes," I replied, "with everything."

And suddenly I saw it all; a lesson there for me.
That "sacred" fence had lost its power; it was plain to see,
that I denied myself a chance to think objectively,
because I let what-always-was dictate what-had-to-be.

Gordon demonstrated wisdom; breaking from the norm;
that what you see from where you are might only be a form
that changes, varies, opens doors to different points of view.
I vowed that when I looked at fields, I'd take out fences too.

I had learned a lesson that I never would forget.
I tend to see the customary, common way, and yet,
when now I see a field of life, a thought in me commences,
I see the field, what it can be, when I remove the fences.

"You cut the fence!" I blurted out, "You ruined it you know."

THE HOUSE WITH A PURPLE DOOR

Villanelle #13

In the eyes of the world, it was just a shack,
the little house with a purple door.
He said, "Mama, when are we going back?"

They had left their home by the railroad track
about a year before.
In the eyes of the world it was just a shack.

His mother was suddenly taken aback
by the little boy about four.
He said, "Mama, when are we going back?"

They had bought a big house with a lot of jack,
but that purple door house he adored.
In the eyes of the world it was just a shack,

but to him, it was a home without lack,
where they lived by the track before.
He said, "Mama, when are we going back?"

He started to pack his little backpack
to return to his home, oh so poor.
In the eyes of the world it was just a shack;
he said, "Mama, when are we going back?"

THE HAMMER AND THE AXE

"I want to chop like you, Daddy!
Can I have an axe of my own?"
said a four-year-old, a little laddie,
nowhere near half grown.
"I also want to pound some nails,
so I need a hammer, too.
I'll build a house and cut some rails
when I am big like you."
The little boy was slight and frail,
his daddy wise and kind.
"How could he ever split a rail?"
went through his daddy's mind.
The only nails he saw him use
were fingernails he chewed.
His dad did tell him that abuse
was dirty, wrong and rude;
that he should quit and grow them out.
His fingernails would shine.
The little boy, whose will was stout
would not to that resign.
His daddy offered him a brand
new hammer as a prize'
if nails upon his little hands
would grow to normal size.
And he would get some nails to pound
into the woodshed post.
He'd practice long until he found
his aim was good, almost.
The chewing stopped, his nails grew long,
the boy was proud to show.
The hammer came! His arm grew strong
from swinging blow on blow.
Then he got another prize

for doing what he should.
A little hatchet just his size,
so he could chop some wood.
Day after day he honed his skills,
an expert he became.
When splitting rails it gave him thrills
to think he overcame
that habit as a little lad
of biting fingernails;
a trifling thing, not really bad,
but addiction, life assails.
Then later on his houses came,
he built them strong and true.
And life's temptations, hurt and blame
attacked as they will do.
But he did overcome them all
with power that he learned
when he was very small,
and his daddy was concerned
enough to help him overcome
a habit, teach a skill
to strengthen him and save him from
himself, as daddies will.

*His daddy offered him a brand new hammer as a prize
if nails on his little hands would grow to normal size.*

THE CHRISTMAS FOOTBALL WISH

"Oh Daddy, we would like to have
a football of our own.
We really want to learn to pass and kick.
The Christmas time is coming soon
and we are nearly grown.
Why, I am seven, brother Randy six."
"A football wish is expensive, boys,
and Santa's pretty poor,
but I will ask him what the chances are."
"You might write him a letter, Rex,
and let him know the score.
Old Santa fills his orders from afar."
So Santa got a letter from
two little farmer boys;
their football dreams depended on a ball.
They let him know they didn't long
for any other toys.
Their list to him was very very small.
It simply said, "Dear Santa Claus,
we know it may be hard
for you to bring a football Christmas Eve.
But we are hoping we'll be playing
football in our yard
on Christmas Day. We're trying to believe.
A football is the only thing
we'll need when you come here.

We'd like some other things but we'll not ask.
It must take lots of money for
the presents every year.
We wonder how you manage such a task."
Their daddy read the letter through,
then put it in the mail.
He agonized, not knowing what to do.
Old Santa's funds were running low,
but he just couldn't fail
those little boys, whose wishes were so few.
He talked it over with their Mom,
they made a secret plan.
They'd sell a baby calf they planned to raise,
and help old Santa buy the ball—
he'd surely understand,
why, he might even have a word of praise.
On Christmas Eve while children slept
old Santa did his thing.
Next morning underneath the Christmas tree,
two spellbound children spied the ball!
It made them dance and sing!
Old Santa read their letter, they could see.
They passed and kicked the rubber ball
outside that Christmas Day;
played catch with Daddy in the house at eve.
The blazing fireplace gave them light
so they could see to play—
(one would pass, the other would receive).

At last they tired and went to bed;
the football stayed behind.
But pigskin passes filled their happy dreams.
They also dreamt of Santa Claus,
so thoughtful and so kind.
He honored Christmas wishes to extremes.
Next morn the boys rushed in the living room.
They grabbed their ball and played some catch
with no one in between.
One missed a pass that sealed the football's doom.
It bounced and rolled away from them
behind the fireplace screen.

*They kicked and passed the rubber ball
outside that Christmas Day.*

One ran for Mother yelling for her aid.
"The football's burning up!" he cried.
"Come help us, Mama, quick!"
The other, though he really was afraid,
had made a valiant effort
to retrieve it with a stick.

But there against a piece of burning wood,
was that, which they had waited for
for all of two long years,
a hole burned in its side—it was no good.
They rolled it over. Grief set in.
They both burst into tears.
Their daddy came in from the barn just then.
He gazed upon the saddest scene;
it was a sorry sight.
The boys looked like they'd lost their only friend.
While peering at their ruined ball
he hugged and held them tight.
He knew he had to give the boys new hope.
He said, "I know a man, a vulcanizer,
I will call.
He patches rubber things. Don't cry and mope.
If he can fix an inner tube,
then he might patch your ball."
A hopeful smile spread o'er their tear-stained faces.
"You think it can be fixed?" he heard them say.
He said, "The hole is on the side,
it's not burned on the laces.
We'll see if he can fix it right away."
The vulcanizer did his job,
sealed on the rubber patch.
They pumped it up. Though not as good as new,
it "filled the bill," it was great fun
to punt and pass and catch,

ev'n though it wobbled ev'ry time they threw.

It also leaked a little air—

quite often it went flat.

But pump and needle were always at hand.

So thankful were the little boys,

they didn't care 'bout that.

They had a football! Everything was grand.

"The football's burning up!" he cried.
"Come help us Mama, quick!"

THE SKUNK TRAPPERS

A week at Grandma's house with Cousin Dick
would always prove a wild adventure trip.
The barn, the model T, the drying slough
would stimulate a boy to pack his grip
and dream of fun, and then anticipate
exciting days, the warmth of summer sun;
with Cousin Dick's inventive, open mind
to keep his little cousins on the run.

My Brother, Randy, youngest of us three,
had had a winter trapping line with me.
We caught a coon, and mink; and summer last,
a skunk with chicken loving tendency.
That skunk had really opened up our eyes.
Our chicken eggs were disappearing fast.
His midnight snack was eating laying hens,
'til trapped, and finished with a rifle blast.

Our Grandpa's chickens, always running free,
were easy pickin's for this summer skunk.
The skunks lived in small holes along the bank
where muskrats lived before the slough had shrunk.
The water had gone down, the slough was dry,
where only weeks before we caught fine trout,
chased bullfrogs off the bank to hear them cry,
and paddled Uncle Jim's canoe about.

From Uncle Jim's garage, we sneaked two traps;
we "set" them in the bank, each in a hole,
so when the unsuspecting skunk stepped in a trap
he'd fall out in the slough and probably roll.
Each trap had wires connected to the stake
out in the middle of the dry slough bed.
Excitement kept us from a good nights sleep.
But we could not have guessed what lay ahead.

*Ol' Pepper'n Tige were running up ahead.
With horror, we beheld the worst of dreams.*

When morning came, we grabbed the twenty-two
and hurried out to see what we had caught.
About the time we reached the dried up slough
we re'lized there was something we forgot.
We hadn't tied up either of Grandpa's dogs!
Ol' Pepper'n Tige were running up ahead.
With horror, we beheld the worst of dreams.
They spied two skunks in traps that were not dead.

They sailed into the frey, attacked those skunks.
The traps and wires were one big tangled mess.
We watched in helpless terror as the spray
began to fly, the dogs displayed their great distress
by yelping loudly; rolling in the dirt,
then springing to their feet, they'd charge again
to meet that blinding spray that really hurt
their eyes and noses, stopping them, and then,

assailed the smelly polecats 'til they gained
the upperhand and overcame their stinky foe.
We slowly walked back to the house again
and as we entered Grandma let us know
that we weren't welcome 'til we had a bath.
You see, we'd gotten closer than we thought.
Our clothes were reeking with that dreadful smell.
Both Grandma and we boys were now distraught.

She set two washtubs in the old woodshed.
We filled four pails with water clear and cold
that we had pumped by hand from Grandpa's well.
We filled the washtubs just as we were told.
Grandma said, "Take off those smelly clothes
and jump into the tubs and wash real good."
Oh, how embarrassing it was; stark naked,
in that woodshed without wood! !

We shed our clothes; humiliated boys,
and covering our private parts we slipped
into those icy washtubs for a bath
afraid of someone watching when we stripped.
Our clothes were soaked in some tomato juice
that Grandma squeezed from precious garden fruits.

*We shed our clothes—humiliated boys, and covering our
private parts, we slipped into those icy washtubs for a bath.*

She brought clean clothes we hurriedly put on;
at last, we covered up our birthday suits.
the dogs were banished from the house, also,
for several days, until the scent grew faint.
We boys retired from trapping skunks for good,
with not an ounce of pressure or restraint.

THE CEDAR FOREST

Hunting was important

during those years when money melted into food

for children's hungry mouths.

A well fed buck deer

provided many tasty meals.

But in times of introspection,

I wondered if hunting was an excuse to immerse myself

in the quiet majestic shelter of a

mysterious forest of cedar trees.

I wanted to be there alone.

I had come upon it quite by accident

while hunting and hiking

in an area I thought I knew,

but suddenly my pathway changed magically,

like the melody of a symphony shifting from horns to violins,

as I seemed to walk into another world.

I entered a Cedar Forest,

alongside a sparkling river called the Satsop,

whose water was so clear, you could count the rocks

in its deep riverbed.

This forest had seen no roads or machines,

and, doubtlessly very few men

since it sprang forth

about 75 years before, as eager seedlings.
Its natural re-growth became an enchanting accomplishment.
The new crop had grown to where
the trees were about 150 feet tall
with diameters between one-and-a-half and two feet,
standing close together.
Their entwining crowns formed an irregular,
lacy, dark green pattern against a blue sky,
blotting out all but struggling streams of sunlight.
Their lower limbs had died and broken off
from ground level up to about 50 to 75 feet above the ground.
When I was walking through the forest,
there was almost no sound if I stayed on
the light green carpet of moss,
or followed the hoof-worn deer trails
and stepped between the dead boughs
cast to the forest floor by Nature's pruning winds.
It seemed as if I had left
the real world of work,
responsibility, and worry,
to find myself under a protecting canopy
of stillness.
Solitude and beauty would wrap their loving arms
around me as I stood unmoving,

tasting the pleasantly pungent cedar-influenced air,

that caused a delightfully tingling sensation in my nostrils.

The cathedral-like atmosphere

promoted a reverence I had never experienced outside before.

It seemed as if God had made that special place,

and it was so wonderful

He lingered to enjoy it Himself.

His presence was always there.

I received much more pleasure

from experiencing it's magic enchantments through the years,

than from the several nice bucks

I took from its cover.

It seemed as if I had left the real world of work, responsibility, and worry, to find myself under a protecting canopy of stillness.

THANKSGIVING DAY

Turkey on tap

a leisurely nap

potatoes mashed

pumpkin smashed

pilgrim stories

Father's glories

from above

family love

cousins playing

Daddy praying

home from college

spewing knowledge

cell phones say

from far away

"Wish I were Home

Thanksgiving Day."

Cell phones say from far away, "Wish I were home Thanksgiving Day."

PERFECT COMMUNICATION

Old Tag and Nig, Dad's skillful team of horses were the best;
or so he thought, they always seemed one cut above the rest.
Two thousand pounds, a dapple gray, Dad's fav'rite was old Tag.
When pulling heavy loads away his gut would nearly drag.
I watched, though I was just a lad and no experience I had
to judge the feelings of a horse. But when I sensed my Dad enforce
his thoughts and wishes of the course old Tag should pull the wagon through
by softly clucking, whistle sucking, pulling lines, he gave the clue.
So Tag would lead without Nig bucking in the harness as they drew
the wagon 'cross the rushing stream o're slip'ry rocks, his feet were sure,
wide Belgian hooves that gripped, it seemed,
inspiring Nig, though insecure to spawn his best expenditure,
I tuned my spirit to the waves twixt horse and man where faith was king,
exuding secret silent raves. My Dad had hardly said a thing.
Though in my youth, the silent call from man to beast excited me.
I didn't understand it all but knew it wasn't fantasy.
Throughout my life I gently stored connecting silent thoughts so free;
that spirit line, that endless chord that stretches to eternity.

Guest Artist
Brady Erickson

I turned my spirit to the waves 'twixt horse and man where faith was king,
exuding secret silent raves. My dad had hardly said a thing.

SUMMER FARM SCENES FROM OUR TEENS

A dairy farm conjures up stories and scenes.
Randy and I had progressed to our teens.
Four-forty-five the alarm clock rings.
We leap from our bed as if we had springs.
Daddy is leaving his bedroom downstairs.
We never took time for scriptures or prayers,
for we didn't know Heavenly Father back then,
still, Daddy did teach us just how to be men.

We went to the bathroom, then threw on our pants
and ran down the stairs. It wasn't by chance
that we were on time for the cow-milking chore.
The milk truck would be there by seven, or before.
Each one did his job as set out by our dad.
By working together it wasn't so bad,
in fact, we enjoyed it, the cattle were fun,
the mornings were fresh, awaiting the sun.

Mom's breakfast was lavish with all we could eat,
of bacon, fried eggs, hotcakes, cream of wheat;
or oatmeal, or French toast, or sausage, or ham;
rice crispies, or cornflakes, or wheaties or spam.
Of course we were hungry from that early start.
We never had coffee or tea; Dad was smart.
No stimulant needed to open the day,
adrenaline helped us to get underway.

Those warm summer days spurred the best in us all.
Each day there were projects, extensive or small.
The number one job was to store winter feed.
With milk cows and young stock we had a great need.

The way we milked cows in earlier days.

In earlier days we would harvest the hay
using horse-drawn mower and rake in a way
that left fluffy straight windrows of quick drying grass
that we'd shock with our pitchforks (piles we'd amass).
Those shocks would be pitched on the wagon just right
where the "loader" would spread, pack, and tie it down tight,
so it wouldn't slide off on its ride up the lane
to the barn; how our horses in harness would strain.
We would park the hay load by the barn at the end
where the loader would ready the hay to ascend.
We'd unhook the horses and drive them around
to the barn's other end where a cable was wound
through a series of blocks to pull up the hay.
Old Nig was a black and Old Tag dapple-gray.
We'd hook on the horses and wait for a yell.
"Go ahead," said the "loader;" the horses could tell,

*We would park the hay load by the barn at the end
where the loader would ready the hay to ascend.*

they should carefully pull on the cable until
the hay reached the block and rolled in on a rail.
The man in the mow would yell, "tripper!" The team
would immediately stop when they heard that loud scream.
The "loader" would jerk on the trip rope; the hay
would drop where the mower would spread it away.
But farming, back then, was much harder it seemed.
The new innovations were more than we'd dreamed.

A tractor for horses, and milking machines;
a pump in a well replaced water from springs.
Electric lights came on by flipping a switch.
A powered machine for digging a ditch.

We filled the tall silo with clover and grass
that we chopped up real fine and blew in en-mass.
The loft in the barn was piled high with baled hay
for the cattle to eat on a cold winter's day.

New fences were built, irrigation was changed,
the machinery repaired, and the shop rearranged.
The pastures were clipped, the manure was spread,
the barns were all cleaned and the chickens were fed.
When it looked like there wasn't a thing left to do,
we'd run over something and break it in two,
then fix and repair time would take up the day,
just when we were thinking of resting, or play.
But nothing compares to the lessons we learned
as we worked and we overcame problems that burned
some indelible answers and methods within,
to give us the knowledge and power to win
as we met life headlong in our quest for success
as adults, in a world where we sought happiness.

And it wasn't all work! Dad knew how to play.
When he couldn't do it he thought of a way;
he worked overtime, he picked up our chores,
so we could play basketball, football, outdoors,
and badminton, ping pong, and checkers inside.
His sacrifice taught us respect, thanks, and pride.
He took us to games at the school when he could.
He coached us, encouraged us how to "get good."
We learned to compete, do our best, try to win.
But if we were beaten, get up, try again.

At times the day lingered, it seemed slow to end.
Milk cows morn and evening, day work to attend.
But it was not boring, we seldom got tired.
We never did worry that we might be fired.

And after our suppertime (evening meal)
we played with our neighbor boys, or took our creel
and fishing pole down to the river that flowed

all along the east side of our farm near the road.
The water was therapy, cool on our feet.
At breakfast next morning we had trout to eat.

There were no vacations for Dad from our farm
no beach to relax on without the alarm
that he strangled each morning before it could ring.
He never complained about missing a thing,
though a person for people he certainly was,
the life of a party, a great Santa Claus.
There were those occasions he took Mom away,
but seldom stayed more than a night and a day.
Randy and I milked the cows, did the chores.
But Dad kept control of the whys and wherefores.

After suppertime we took our creel and fishing pole down to the river.
At breakfast next morning we had trout to eat.

He made sure we got to the 4-H club camp
for a week every year, although it would cramp
him and make his days long, he seemed to enjoy
helping us to have fun like he did, as a boy.

Dad wanted us boys to be prosperous and great.
He laid the foundation; had patience to wait.
He taught us good principles; to think, concentrate.
To be there on time; not procrastinate.
But sometimes we failed when we had work to do;
not follow directions and make a miscue.
He was a taskmaster, expected a lot,
would criticize loudly a plea, "I forgot."
He had a bad temper when things would go wrong,
so nobody crossed him; they knew he was strong.
And when he got mad he would say a bad word,
but we boys pretended that we hadn't heard
for we never swore, or drank coffee or beer.
We honored Dad's wishes, (it could have been fear)

Some cool summer evenings when day's work was done
we'd lap up Mom's tastiest supper, bar none,
and move to the living room sofas and chairs,
Where we'd sing and make music, forgetting our cares.
With Mother's piano and Daddy's guitar
we'd sing the old songs like a Grand Opry star.

Our bedtime was early and so was our rise.
Good health we had, surely, but wealthy and wise
were things in the future. Foundation we had;
thanks to the efforts of Mother and Dad.

And so went those great summer days in our teens.
We saved up our pennies so we'd have the means
to go on to college, a business, or trade;
to step out with confidence, not be afraid.
Our work habits, farm education complete,
we looked for exciting horizons to greet.

THE WILD STEER HUNT

In looking back recalling years spent on our valley farm,
a wild steer hunt comes into mind. With rifles on our arms,
I trudged with Dad o'er "hill and dale" one Friday morn in fall.
We early milked our herd of cows, fed calves and bull and all.
Anticipation of this trip had piqued our minds for days.
Three Holstein steers, now four years old had gotten wild and crazed.

Our cattle went on open range when young, in budding spring
ten thousand acres logged off land, no roads or anything.
No poacher's truck could enter in; the cattle grazed in peace
from Satsop to Wynooche Rivers, Dad acquired a lease.
The stumps and logs were black from fires, young trees just seedlings then,
and we could see a mile from hilltops o'er the grassy glens.
Dad's friends that farmed the Satsop side would watch our cattle there,
and they had livestock of their own, our pasture they would share.
Before the chilly days and nights when grass would cease to grow,
each farmer drove his cattle home to care for them and know
that they would have some hay to eat when bitter winds would blow;
in a barn made warm with body heat, a shelter from the snow.

Some animals would not come in when winter-time was nigh.
If they remained out in those hills, most often they would die.
The Holstein steers I mentioned here hid out at round-up time.
They found a marsh where elk and deer survived the frigid clime.
They broke the ice on shallow ponds to eat the grass beneath
and watercress and other greens—they somehow cheated death.
When sent into the hills as calves, those steers were nice and tame.
Each winter spent away from home, the wilder they became.

We tried to bring them in each fall, but when we ventured near
they bolted for the swamps up north, to live with elk and deer.
They got so wild and smart; it seemed, their senses were acute
and they could run for miles on end, each time a different route.

This morning Dad and I hiked in for six or seven miles.
We met three Satsop Valley men with greetings hushed, and smiles.
The cattle herd was bedded down, the steers lay in their midst.
The men had seen them coming in, Kriss Muller and the Schmitz.
Those cattle were on the valley floor, the river on the east.
The other sides were like a bowl, up fifty feet at least.
We all spread out along each ridge, surrounding the resting herd.
My Dad was picked to stalk the prey. He left without a word.
He sneaked down to the valley floor behind some brush and stumps,
to cross the several hundred yards in runs and crawls and jumps.
When half-way there, the steers sprang up, for they had heard him move.
Their heads were high; they looked for him, Dad's sight of them improved.
He aimed his 30 Remington, a log would brace it still.
The steer went down; we heard a crack and knew he had a kill.
The other steers, disorganized, befuddled, milled around.
They didn't know which way to run, their leader on the ground.
One steer saw Dad and stared at him. Dad quickly aimed and shot.
The steer went down, but jumped right up! Dad had missed the spot.
The bullet entered on his nose, too low to reach the brain.
He took off running, stumbling, falling over rough terrain.
He started up the hill where on the ridge Kriss Muller stood.
Kriss waited till the steer was close, stepped out to see him good.
When he was twenty feet away, Kriss raised the gun to shoot.
His semi-automatic thirty-two should stop the brute.

He pulled the trigger--no report. The charging steer was crazed!
Kriss quickly dove into the brush, the steer went on unfazed.
The gun had jammed and Kriss was lucky to evade the charge.
The trail was narrow where he stood, the animal so large.
I watched just up the ridge from Kriss, but didn't get a shot,
so hurried to meet up with him, for happy he was not.
That steer was wounded badly though, for his trail was easy seen.
He floundered through the briars and thorns, left blood spots red on green.
Kriss Muller said he'd help my Dad dress out the steer he got,
and Badger Schmitz would help him too, yes Dad was one crack shot.
They told me Elton Schmitz and I should trail the wounded steer
for he would surely stop and die not very far from here.

Now, Elton Schmitz was six-feet-two and twenty-five years of age,
while I was twelve, weighed 80 pounds, and on a different page.
I soon became aware I took two steps to Elton's one.
He strode right out with big long legs—to keep up I would run.
The time was ten A. M. when we began to chase that steer.
We couldn't seem to gain on him, but we did persevere.
He crashed through thickets, prickly spruce, and stands of devil's clubs.
His trail was easy followed, he left blood on bush and shrubs.
It soon was noon, we couldn't stop to eat our carried lunch,
or even stop to rest a bit 'cause we both had a hunch
that we should never let his trail get cold or he might hide
and die before we found him, though we'd hunt him far and wide.

He traveled north toward the swamps, through places new to me.
I got so tired, lagged behind, now it was half past three.
My legs like lead, I told my friend that I could run no more.
He said, "I think we'll catch him if you can just go till four."

So I drug on and forced myself. At four o'clock I stopped.
"I can't go any farther," I told Elton, then I dropped.
"I've never seen this place before, I don't know where I am."
He said, "Rest up and get your wind." He drew a diagram
in soft fresh dirt with pointed stick. "You head out that-a-way.
You need to walk toward that hill, about a mile, I'd say.
When you get there you'll find a trail that you should recognize.
Go east and cross the river, look around and scrutinize.
I think you'll find your way to Kriss's farm before it's dark.
I'll follow this wild steer until my bullet finds its mark."

I rested up and ate a bite of lunch for energy,
then grabbed my gun and off I trudged. I hoped that I would see
familiar ground before too long, and have vitality
to walk the last three miles alone. It would be hard for me.
Alone. I really felt alone. But I must be a man.
I'd had good training in the woods. I had a walking plan.
I was five-foot-one or two, my body lean and strong.
At twelve years old, convinced my Dad that I should go along
when he went out to get the steers. Now I must pass my test.
I had to keep directions sure, go south and east not west.
The hill that Elton pointed to, I kept within my sight,
and made myself keep up the pace to reach the farm by night.

Four thirty came. I reached the hill. I finally heard a shot.
I later learned that Elton had increased his speed and caught
up to the wounded steer and shot him on a road.
He hailed a ride that took him to Kriss Muller's farm abode.
They used a sled to haul him to the barn and dress him out.
The first steer shot was hanging there. All were glad, no doubt.

Meanwhile, I struggled valiantly to somehow make it back.
I found the trail and crossed the river, had a final snack.
The last two miles my feet hurt so and night was coming on.
But, thankfully I reached the barn, then all my strength was gone.
For I had hiked for fifteen miles, or more, since early dawn.
The ground was rough, much up and down, not like a field or lawn.

Our Mother came and drove us home; the hunt for steers was through.
My Daddy milked our cows by hand, and he was tired too.
My brother, Randy did his part, but I soon went to bed
with thoughts and dreams of those wild steers resounding in my head.

Guest Artist
Brady Erickson

He pulled the trigger—no report.
The charging steer was crazed! Kriss quickly dove into the brush,
the steer went on unfazed.

THE VALENTINE ADVENTURE

We were so poor when we began
to see ourselves as woman and man.
The phone calls and the precious hours
when talk was fresh as rain-splashed flowers.
The fun, the love, and then the laughter,
recipes for life thereafter.
You were so young and thought me wise,
an older man, who could advise
you, as you met the wiley world,
adventures only at you hurled
if you should choose to stick with me,
a curious adventuree.
And now as many years have passed
you're still expecting first and last
the unknown tricks of Father Time
to touch your life and make it rhyme
with me, my love, because you're mine,
a tried and loving Valentine.

THE GRANDEST GRANDKIDS

Our Grandkids certainly are fun.
But, then, there is that special one
who never fails to cause a fuss
when they come up to visit us.
The kid unties his Grandma's strings
and tries to hang on her earrings.
Her apron falls below her knees,
her ears resemble high trapeze.
That Grandson is a winsome lad,
who really isn't all that bad,
but when a cousin happens by
he picks a fight; we don't know why.
They punch and wrestle recklessly
and roll into the Christmas tree.
Ornaments, of course, are broken,
angry words from Grandma spoken.
Things are calm about a minute,
after that they're right back in it,
running all around the house,
jumping on the chairs and couch,
flying as in outer space
crashing down on Grandma's vase.
When Grandma can't take anymore
there enters three more through the door.

She calls for help and Grandpa hears.
(He's been hiding from their spears
and swords) but he comes out,
trying not to yell and shout.
He gives those kids just one more chance
before he warms their underpants.
Things are quiet for a moment,
Then they find a new component.
Older cousins happen in
so now they're up and off again.
They're rolling, rumbling, being loud,
and there is now a bigger crowd.
"Its TV time," their Grandma yells,
"Stow your whistles, trucks and bells
into the cupboards 'long the wall.
Hey you! Don't throw that basketball!!
Come on now, pick up the toys
and act like proper girls and boys."
They finally start to settle down
and watch a show of great renown;
a film for kids that teaches how
to fight and bite and sock, "kerpow!!"
That makes it really hard to win.
You know they're coming back again
and they'll be fresh with all those tricks
they learned. Their swords they

make from sticks

to hit and knock each other down!

It's good we have TV around, (???)

so they can learn to fight and scrap.

That television is a trap.

But they'll grow up. I'll never fear

because of super parents dear,

Who'll slowly teach them right from wrong,

to mind, to love, to get along.

Yes we'll be pleased at what they do,

how they develop brave and true.

Now time is marching swiftly on.

It won't be long until they're gone

and we will miss them and their fun

til they return with three for one.

... running all around the house, jumping on the chairs and couch, flying as in outer space, crashing down on Grandma's vase.

BILLIE JEAN

We started school when I was six; there was no kindergarten then;
a motley bunch of kids, a mix from every cage, corral, and pen.
We had a red haired teacher, who was dedicated to our gain.
Miss Hunt would teach us all to do our math, and we read "Dick and Jane."

I had few playmates up till then, but from them I had learned some things,
that some were nice from start to end, but there were those who left their stings.
Some were pretty, like a queen; those girls would take my longest thought;
above all, one named Billie Jean, who acted nice, and never fought.

Her head was full of golden curls; her smile lit up the room for me.
She wasn't like the other girls, a six year old could even see.
And though she liked me too, I knew, we never made our feelings known.
Then one sad day she moved away, I suddenly felt all alone.

I never knew her smile again; those golden curls I saw no more.
She only moved ten miles, but then, to me, 'twas like ten thousand four.
Now why would she still light my mind? For sixty years have come and gone.
You see, she was a special kind with sunset's peace, and glow of dawn.

Sometimes she walks into my dream, imagination's storybook.
There is no kiss, no touch, no theme, just tossing curls; a loving look.
There is no fierceness in my love, I can't project a final scene.
But thoughts seem sweet when thinking of my first grade girlfriend, Billie Jean.

Now why would she still light my mind?
For sixty years have come and gone.
You see, she was a special kind with
sunset's peace, and glow of dawn.

BE MY GUEST

How many times must I warn you?
How many times can you not hear?
My angels show you what to do,
    but penetrate not your ear.

I do not want to let you go.
You're a precious sheep of my fold,
    but your spirit, free, says no
to me and your mansion made of gold.

I would take you 'neath my wing
    and shelter you from storms.
Oh, child of mine, what is the thing
    to which your heart conforms?

Do you not know, I'm just inside
    the door; why won't you knock?
I'll open it if you'll abide
    with me; there is no lock.

The choices you have made so far,
    not always have been best.
Your conscience tells me who you are;
    will you not be my guest?

For I am He who will forgive
    those moments in your past,
wherein you slipped and didn't live
    my guidelines to the last.

If you repent, I will forget
    the times you went astray.
But please forgive yourself, and let
    my Spirit have its way.

SLIPPING FROM WORK TO REST

Sonnet #1

To know the secret of a true repose

when batt'ling will, resisting time to rest;

my mind, a door that seems to never close

spews gems of new ideas with great zest.

The muscles of my brain, a state of flex;

why is it? I should revel in the chance

to put my feet up; loosening complex

and choking belts, my freedoms to enhance.

Alas, sometimes I fail to see just why

the motor of my mind keeps running on,

forgetting that the time is passing by

to slip from work to rest before I'm gone.

But God provides no pattern for relief

from life, or work, or love, is my belief.

DEAR AUNTIE IS OLDER

Villanelle #1

She was always so loving to me;
though married, no child of her own.
Dear Auntie is older and soon will be free.

Coats for her nephews, how lucky were we,
they were perfectly fitted and sewn.
She was always so loving to me.

Dresses and dolls for her nieces with glee
she would sew, up all night all alone.
Dear Auntie is older and soon will be free.

Who was her favorite? I thought it was me.
But I wonder, now that I'm grown.
She was always so loving to me.

It seems that each niece thought it was she.
Each nephew thought he her gemstone.
Dear Auntie is older and soon will be free.

Now she is older! There's no rivalry,
her feebleness we will enthrone.
She was always so loving to me.
Dear Auntie is older and soon will be free.

COUSIN DICK AND THE RIVER'S PERIL

Whenever I retreat in thought to relive days gone by,
My mind recaptures pleasant times when I would dream
to be like "fearless" Cousin Dick who came from Aberdeen.
He'd visit us out on the farm and liven up the scene.

Our pretty little dairy farm was well controlled by Dad.
But Cousin Dick could change the pace—which was both good and bad.
Wynooche River Valley boys were known for steadfast ways.
When work was done we had our fun and so we filled our days.

But Cousin Dick could think of things that none of us had thought;
and yet we stayed in harmony and never ever fought.
He lived beside the tidal flats. On homemade rafts he sailed.
While very young he learned to swim because his boats had failed.

He loved the water and the wilds, adventure was his lot.
Although he sometimes disobeyed, a bad boy he was not.
His curiosity was great, excitement he could find.
And when he took us boys along we knew he would be kind.

We had the river through our farm, a wondrous place to play.
When I was six and he was eight, he came to spend the day.
His mother and my mom said, "To the river---DO NOT GO!"
But Cousin Dick could not resist the water with its flow.

In summertime the river seemed so peaceful and so tame.
The swimming hole, the sparkling riffles, fish and fowl and game.
But wintertime with days of rain, the river changed its mind.
It's swollen waters racing down to see what it could find.

He took me and my brother Randy, who was only four,
And slid us down the river bank where we could hear the roar
of water as it rushed along nearly at our feet.
Then little Randy slipped and fell, down upon his seat,

And slid out in the swollen stream---but as he drifted by
our Cousin Dick just plucked him out. While Randy didn't cry,
he still was wet and cold and tried to climb back up the bank.
He slipped and slid back in the stream, but just before he sank,

We pulled him from the muddy drink to safety once again,
and pushed him up the slippery bank, right to the top and then----
he slipped again and down he came out in the water cold.
But Dick and I reached for his arms and finally got a hold.

This time Dick pushed me up the bank and as I held a tree,
he lifted Randy up until he got a hold of me.
I pulled him up to safety and Dick climbed up alone.
We all were pretty wet by then as we set out for home.

When we came in and Mother saw her little boys were wet,
we realized the river's peril was not completed yet.
Although she was extremely glad that we lived through our trip,
we didn't see that happy face when she laid on the whip.

A mother's love is fierce sometimes when using Daddy's belt,
but I was sad that Cousin Dick did not receive one welt!
His mother said, "Why Dick, you shouldn't take those boys down there."
And that was it. I realized then that life just wasn't fair.

Well, maybe I'd be braver too, without the spanking threat.
His mother cared but had a different way of showing it.
I still was happy Mother Dear, could teach me right from wrong,
but when our Cousin said, "Let's go!" we'd gladly tag along.

CEDAR CREEK, THE ENCHANTED STREAM

"Is it a river, or a brook?"

The question you might weigh.

The answer rests on when you look,

post winter storms, or summer day.

In winter, water wends its way

with wildly whirling waves.

Its murky torrents on display,

the river misbehaves.

But summer settles like a psalm

and soothes the surging stream.

The rainstorms cease, the skies are calm,

the sun regains its self-esteem.

The brilliance of emerging green

is everywhere you look,

and cutthroat trout are often seen

as they attack a hook.

The water sparkles in the sun,

with beauty clean and clear.

The brook is born. The river done,

till winter sheds its tear.

THE MODEL T FORD

The Model T was in the barn for many many years,
its motor silent; rusting, tires flat,
with chickens roosting on the steering wheel, above its gears
that hadn't meshed or turned, just simply sat.
The chickens, known as Plymouth Rocks, were black with speckles white.
They roamed the barnyard freely every day.
But when the sun set in the west to threaten with the night,
the Model T was where they flew to stay.
Accumulated chicken droppings from their roosting spots
just piled a little higher every year.
So when our Cousin Dick was entertaining driving thoughts,
he made his smaller cousins volunteer
to be the chicken poop removers, clean the rusting truck,
oh yes, and throw the hay out of the bed;
where hens had fluffed and nested, laid their eggs with many-a-cluck
and hatched their baby chickens, Grandpa said.

The second war with Germany was in its bloody height;
my Uncle Frank was called from Grandpa's ranch.
He left that peaceful farm to join the Navy, go and fight.
A carrier for aircraft was his branch.

Our Cousin Dick was twelve, while I was ten and Randy eight.
We wanted so to drive that Model T.
We tried to get it started; We pushed and pulled that crate.
We cranked and cranked it 'til we couldn't see.
But Uncle Jim had mentioned that it might have been the coil.
We needed to remove it, give it heat.
So Grandma's wood stove oven where she put her steaks to broil
was used to warm the coil instead of meat.
It seemed to energize it, though I really don't know why,

but then the motor seemed to want to start.
We propped the gas tank up on blocks behind the seat, up high,
so fuel would drain into the engine's heart.
We tried all settings of the throttle handle and the spark
while Dick turned o'er the motor with the crank,
when suddenly it sputtered, coughed and made a loud remark
and started!! We could not begin to thank
our lucky stars enough, our dream was really coming true.
That truck had found "go potion" in its tank.
That Model T had come to life anew!
We patched the inner tubes and pumped the tires up by hand
Our "maiden voyage" was soon to come to pass.

We opened up the barnyard gate and gazed across the land.
There stretched before us open prairie grass.
Then Dick released the hand brake while he pulled the throttle down.
We crossed the county road into the field.
Then out across the wide expanse; no fence, no tree, nor town.
It seemed we felt the world around us yield.
The prairie where we picked wildflowers: buttercups, blue bells,
and violets for Grandma, days before,
had lost its flower magic, now was casting different spells,
as Dick pulled down the throttle towards the floor.
To us it seemed we fairly flew at thirty miles per hour.
In time we came upon a gravel pit.
We tried to climb the walls, too steep; the motor lost its power.
It took reverse to get us out of it.
For, with the engine higher than the gas tank in the back,
we stalled; that gas just wouldn't run up hill.
But in reverse it worked just fine if we stayed on the track,
so Dick could back it out with little skill.
Then out across the level wide expanse we charged again.
This time I drove the crazy old machine.

I learned to drive our '37 Ford at home by then,
but this was diff'rent, it was not routine.
We didn't think our Grandma knew that we were "out of bounds",
and Grandpa went to work with Uncle Jim.
But now I realize she surely heard the engine sounds
and worried that our safety would look grim,
especially if she had seen us race that Greyhound bus,
while bumping o'er the prairie 'long the road.
The passengers looked startled as they pulled away from us.
But then they laughed at this strange episode.
If Grandma could have seen us, as Dick drove out in the slough
with water splashing o'er the running boards
she would have wrung her hands and cried, "Oh what am I to do?
The boys are going to sink that Model T Ford."
But then, we all survived our trips,
and we didn't hurt the truck.
We just were glad we coaxed the thing to run.
And though we tempted fate at times we never got it stuck.
That week at Grandma's certainly was fun.

...if Grandma had seen us race that Greyhound bus,
while bumping o're the prairie 'long the road.

THE MASTER MIND

A brilliant star up in the sky-
a brilliant mind to wonder why.
A river flows perpetually
ev'n though it's eaten by a sea.
A bird is flying in the air,
how is man to journey there?
A heart is beating in a chest,
when is the time it comes to rest?
For everything that we uncover,
every thing that we discover
in this world for all mankind
was made ahead for us to find.
Our inspiration's key unlocks
each secret just like building blocks.
Each invention we discover
leads us on to find another.

The patterns we begin to see
were first developed spiritually.
So as we "tune in" with our thoughts,
following the trail of dots
our Maker left for us to find,
we slowly build our master-mind.
It's plain to see it's one big plan
inspiring wonders "made by man,"
which though they be minute or tall,
man really "made them" not at all.

THE SIMPLE PRAYER

We do not need trumpets or edicts from kings

to open the heavens above.

We don't need an earth quake, or other harsh things

to know with a sureness, His love.

We know all it takes is a prayer of the meek,

in humbleness, earnestness, said,

to open the heavens, inspire as we seek,

and are filled with His life giving bread.

WHERE IS PEACE?

The wonders of the universe are constantly evolving.

The changes of the changes never cease.

Though man continues study and is ever problem, solving,

the problem no one solves is "Where is Peace?"

Peace has fewer armies that hide along its shores,

than all the roguish nations of the earth.

So when it came to battles, peace has lost its wars

and waits for man to spawn a great rebirth.

Time has come for allies to rally 'round the cross,

to look for peaceful power over sin.

Then, when it is over, Satan won't be boss,

for man will win the conflict from within.

His peace blooms like a flower, projecting from each heart,

and goodness shows it's great and glorious hand.

Then God will wield his power and all will do their part

to keep the peace with Brotherhood of man.

THE TIP

As soon as I receive the slip

my wife says, "Honey, leave a tip.

Now, leave a big one too. That gal

works hard...I'm sure she needs a pal.

She never smiled one time tonight,

so someone has to treat her right."

In shock I start to bite my lip!

Upon my shirt a gravy drip—

on my radar she is a blip.

Just why should I leave her a tip?

Dear Wifey notices my gloom

(began when she came in the room

and spilt the water in my lap…

I still can feel my wet fly flap.)

At first I tried to cheer her up,

but when she slopped my coffee cup

I saw her mouth and shoulders droop

until her hair drug through my soup!

I just can't help remembering

my steak looked like some dried up thing,

while I, as hungry as a bear,

had told her, "Make it very rare."

I'm sure it was an anklebone

from some poor starving steer, half grown.

I guess I shouldn't give her blame

for meat that suffered too much flame,

but when she argued, "It looks good,"

that wrinkled, tasteless piece of wood

had lost all value to my diet,

it was hard to keep me quiet.

I force myself to grimly smile;

and count my wallet "ones" a while.

I fluff them up to make a pile

look big instead of single file.

It's hard for me to pay her for

incompetence. She makes me sore!

But as I glance at my dear spouse

she winks at me… it's hard to grouse,

to see her pretty, hopeful smile…

I throw some more "ones" on the pile.

And as we leave I hear her quip,

"I'm glad you left a healthy tip."

THE WONDER OF LOVE

Villanelle #9

My love, you are so beautiful to me.
Your pretty eyes just sparkle when you smile.
No wonder you're the only one I see.

Our private moments are so heavenly.
You show me love, you make my life worthwhile.
My love, you are so beautiful to me.

Our vows to serve each other are the key,
enticing each to go the extra mile.
No wonder you're the only one I see.

It's often that we seem to disagree,
but never place the other one on trial.
My love, you are so beautiful to me.

If I am ever lost I hope I'll be
alone with you on some deserted isle.
No wonder, you're the only one I'd see.

I love your heart, I love your thoughts, and style.
We seem to compliment so perfectly.
My love, you are so beautiful to me.
No wonder you're the only one I see.

THE DRINKING CONTEST

A warm, sunny, summer day
was perfect for four boys at play.
Cousin Dick and Cousin Larry,
Rex and Randy; all were very
hot and dry from playing hard,
sat and rested in the yard
beneath a loaded cherry tree
on Grandma's farm on Ford's Prairie.

Cousin Dick would show no pity
for his cousin from the city.
Impish pranks he'd sometimes do,
but when they'd come, we never knew.

"I'm thirsty", Dick was heard to say.
The old hand pump, though rusty gray,
perched on the well some feet away
could quench our thirst without delay.
A silver dipper hanging on
a post nearby was never gone.
It beckoned to us, "Fill me up
with clear, cold water you can sup."
Rex worked the handle, pumping fast;
the water gurgled out at last.
Dick filled the dipper to the brim
and then a thought came over him.

*His breath grew short,
his eyes were glassy,
his stomach pooched
like it was gassy.*

"Let's have a drinking contest, now,
come on, Larry, show us how
much water you can really drink.
Larry said, "A lot, I think,"

Dick said, "Well, Larry, you go first
and show us how to quench your thirst."
So Larry eagerly began
to guzzle water from the pan.

He drank, and drank, and drank, and drank;
he drained that dipper in his tank.
His breath grew short, his eyes were glassy,
his stomach pooched like it was gassy.
Then with a groan, he said, "I give;
if I drink more I may not live!"
Cousin Dick retrieved the dipper
put his arm around the tipper,
with a twinkle in his eye;
Larry, thinking he would die;
Dick said, "Larry, you have won!!"
We couldn't beat what you have done.

THE BEAUTY OF A WAVE

Villanelle #17

Can you express the beauty of a wave?
A friendly gesture coming from the heart?
A frame in time that one would like to save.

You walk along, your countenance is grave.
Your friend will wave and happiness will start.
Can you express the beauty of a wave?

The branches of a tree in wind behave
as if they're greeting you; in beauty part.
A frame in time that one would like to save.

The ocean with its surf, a picture gave
of sparkling water falling all apart.
Can you express the beauty of a wave?

A field of golden grain may cause a rave!
It shimmers in the breeze without a chart.
A frame in time that you would like to save.

A pretty girl, whose hand a man can crave,
might greet and stir him up 'til he's not smart.
Can you express the beauty of a wave?
A frame in time that you would like to save.

THE ADDRESS BOOK

In looking through possessions held and cherished many years,
I saw the names so deftly spelled among her souvenirs.
The address book was tattered, torn; it's binding loose and stripped.
So old, its index tabs were worn from hands whose fingers gripped.
At first I tossed it on the pile of things to throw away.
But after just a little while it beckoned me to stay.
I picked it up, sat down to rest, and opened it again.
It seemed that God my efforts blessed, I gazed upon my name.
The page was smudged from many calls and teardrops, I could tell.
She didn't always share her falls, or tell me when she fell.
Her thoughts and prayers had always been for those she loved and served.
From newborn babe to aging man, 'twas more than I deserved.
Yes, there were many other names within that tattered book.
I scanned the pages, said a prayer, then I began to look
at all her friends who'd gone before, in mem'ry some I'd known.
'Twas then I realized much more why she had felt alone.
A line was neatly penciled through the names when they had died.
"Deceased" was written by them too, and droplets where she cried.

Oh Mother, what a loving soul you were. I miss you so.
I know you're on the Savior's roll, you had not far to go
to meet Him at His throne on high; your mansion He's prepared.
Your crown of glory now is nigh because you loved and cared.

The tattered address book, I'll keep, with names of friends you knew.
Then someday in my final sleep I'll meet them all, with you.

THANKSGIVING IN JUNE

"You darn old turkeys, go back home!!"
I heard my Mother say.
She flapped her apron, shooed them from
our yard that summer day.
For they were scratching up her flowers;
Mom had few to spare.
Her yard did suffer when her hours
were filled with work and care.
She was a special woman, who
would cook and sew and can.
She made our clothes; we loved her food,
she truly blessed her man.
The turkeys were a newfound menace
Mr. Lukin grew.
He raised them in his chicken pen as
dairy farmers do.
The fence was low; their wings grew strong,
as practice flights they took,
and sure enough it wasn't long
their little pen forsook.
They quickly marched right down the road
in single turkey file,
flopped o'er our gate, locate, erode
the peony domicile.
They were my mother's flower gems,
so when their stems were snapped
my Mom became a raging femme;
looked for a turkey trap.
I helped my mother chase them out
back down the road they went.

Mother left, I heard her shout,
her anger she did vent.
"Chase those turkeys on back home
where they belong," she yelled.
O.K., Mama," I alone
would do the job, I felt compelled
to drive those turkeys down the road
and frighten them to death.
I chased them toward their wire abode
'til I was out of breath.
I stopped and grabbed a good sized rock
and whizzed it through the air.
I threw it at the little flock

I stopped and grabbed a good sized rock and whizzed it through the air.

to give them all a scare,
to hurry them along their way
so they would not come back.
Then as I watched to my dismay
I sensed a thudding whack.

The biggest turkey toppled o'er
and gave a lifeless twitch.
As I approached he shook once more
and died there in the ditch.
I didn't know just what to do
when I picked up that fowl.
I thought of Mr. Lukin. Through
my mind I heard him growl.
At that point I was frightened, sick.
Reality set in.
I shook! My stomach tightened, quick,
as if I'd done a sin.
I glanced in each direction;
no witnesses were seen.
I had escaped detection; my reputation clean.
So, picking up that turkey bird
I threw him in the brush
and hurried home without a word
to keep that deed hush-hush.
But when I saw my Mother there
she praised me for my work.
She didn't know; I couldn't bear
to say I was a jerk.
Sickness in my tummy welled.
My eyes were filled with tears.
I ran to Mother to be held;
relating all my fears.
She listened kindly, then she said,
"You must relieve your stress.
Go give the bird, though it is dead,
to Lukins, just confess."

"Oh, no, I couldn't do that, Mom,
I don't know what he'd do.
And when he sees that turkey tom,
killed from a rock I threw
he'll be so mad he'll yell at me,
and maybe hit me too.
I just can't do it. I can't go-
unless I go with you."
My Mother said she'd go along
and listen to me talk.
But I must tell him what was wrong-
it was a painful walk.
I pulled the turkey from the brush.
we strode on up the road.
This eight year old was in no rush
to reach his quaint abode.
The gate, the porch; knocked on the door;
I hoped he wasn't there.
It opened. I had heretofore
been trying to prepare.
But now, I blurted out the words,
"Hi Mr. Lukin here—"
I handed him his biggest bird.
I tried to make it clear.
"He dug in Mama's flower bed.
I chased him out, you see.
I threw a rock and he fell dead.
Please, don't be mad at me!"
Old Mr. Lukin took the bird
and realized my fright.
"Twas hard believing what I heard,
"Thas a'right, thas a'right.

Ve eat him for dinner today," he said.
My heart within me cheered.
I told myself no need to dread.
It wasn't like I feared.
My mother gave a knowing smile
as we turned 'round to go.
But as for me, it took a while.
Recovery was slow.
We visited as home we went,
my Mother made it clear.
Adversity and real torment
bring courage, conquer fear.
And always tell the truth each time
what e'er the circumstance.
Don't hide your turkey; face your crime.
The good life you'll enhance.

Now I blurted out the words, "Hi, Mr. Lukin here—"
I handed him the biggest bird.

THE MEDICARE BAND AT THE NURSING HOME

We set up microphones for six;

one had a music stand.

Our members were a motley mix,

known as The Medicare Band.

Our songs, as old as we, and more,

would fall on ears of age.

They had heard these songs before;

no need for book or page.

The wheel-chairs gathered 'round the room,

the nurses helped them park.

To take away the practiced gloom

were those whose nature sparked.

We sang and played the violins,

the banjo, harp, guitars.

When we were through, applause and grins

would tell us we were stars.

"You made me feel so happy

when you sang for us today.

If it was slow or snappy

I just loved it any way."

So said a voice so cheery

as she reached out for my hand.

Her shining eyes were teary

like she'd been in Wonderland.

I took her hand; we talked a bit,

about her fav'rite song.

My hand, she held tight, wouldn't quit,

but I had to move along.

Here came more wheel-chairs moving slow,

they formed a crooked line.

I sensed they wouldn't let me go

without their hand in mine.

When I conversed with one of them,

the others' courage rose.

They saw that I would not condemn

defects they might disclose.

They reached for love to get, and give

by clinging to my hand,

to show their hope that they could live,

and complement our band.

Most everyone had crippled arms

or legs, or twisted feet.

In younger days with grace and charms
they danced to any beat.
But now, songs they had memorized
were still deep down inside.
When hearing as we harmonized
left many misty-eyed.

"Oh, thank you sir", I heard one say,
"my mouth framed every word.
Those memories you stirred today
were sweet—so glad I heard."
Though some were ill and couldn't speak,
their eyes said loving things.
Their hands, though frail, and sometimes weak,
disclosed a heart that sings.

Our hearts were touched, emotions welled,
we shed a tear or two.
The smiles prevailed, gloom was dispelled,
it warmed us through and through.

An hour from our busy day
was not a sacrifice.
The love we shared, I have to say,
was warm, was good, was nice.

THE PRUNER

The limbs of the half-grown apple tree were grotesque at their best.
The orchard owner didn't see and prune it like the rest.
It sat alone; had never grown the way of other trees
that he had planted row by row and shaped them; eyes to please.
The tangled mess of branches fought their way to see the light.
Till they had hurt themselves, were caught with nothing growing right.

And then one day the orchardist thought he'd remove the tree.
He'd cut it down with axe he brought, "It won't be missed," thought he.
It's apples, tiny, not the size the market did require.
The orchardist had deemed it wise the tree should just expire.

He raised his axe to cut it down but something made him stop.
He looked it over, once around from bottom to the top.
"Oh, what if I remove the wood? (some limbs it doesn't need);
to shape the tree 'til it looks good. It's from the choicest seed."
So he began to prune and trim until the task was done.
It seemed the tree smiled back at him, as it soaked in the sun.

Next year the apples on the tree were bigger than before.
And each succeeding year would see it ripen more and more.

The tree is like an untrained youth whose life is "on the line".
Though he be rash, at times uncouth, and no one's valentine,
when pruned by love and discipline sometimes he will respond.
If in the light his heart is won, to goodness he will bond.
Sometimes we overlook a jewel whose life's a tangled mess?
Who really won't be mean and cruel if we show love, and bless.

So let us watch and be aware of those who most reject,
and ready be to "just be there" to show them our respect.
They, like the tree, will blossom more when pure light filters in.
And help them prune the dross before they're cut off; lost to men.

THE BOUQUET OF LIFE

The budding bouquet was beautiful when it arrived one day.
She put it on the windowsill, the vase which braced its stay
did complement the colors, too, the reds, the greens, the gold,
meshed with that pretty vase of blue, so lovely to behold.

Each day when she came in the room her passion for them rose.
Their beauty and their mild perfume in concert did expose
the youthful freshness of the flowers.
They were so alive,
that she could sense and so devour their will to live and thrive.

The buds were opening; each blossom spread into its space.
The picture made by them was awesome, filled the pretty vase.

As time did quietly roll on there came a subtle change.
Some flowers withered, were far-gone. Those left, she rearranged.

So soon, all flowers met their end, all brilliant colors gone,
except the vase, a minuend of beauty, lingered on.

How sad it was for her to face the loss of vibrant blooms.
For now, no beauty with its grace will cheer her naked rooms.

There is a similarity, the bouquet's life and ours.
When young we reach a parity where we're as fresh as flowers.
Surroundings soon become our vase to hold us straight and true.
(Still, not everybody's place is painted pretty blue.)

But as we age, our bodies and minds do show the test of time.
We live, we love, but each one finds that final hill to climb.

Then one by one we all must fade and they must lay us by.
Like flowers, most are not afraid, we joy in life, then die.

THE DAY WE RANG THE BELL

The Sharon School was closed;
"Consolidated," so they said.
It looked so sad just sitting there;
it's teaching days were dead.

Our Grandma's house across the street
was also old, and dreary.
It never saw a coat of paint
to make it bright and cheery.

But Grandma's home was full of love;
us grandkids liked to stay there.
If only for a week or two
in summer we would play there.

Cousin Dick, with Brother Randy
made our visits fun.
We'd help our Grandpa milk and feed
'til morning chores were done.

Then Cousin Dick would think and plan
to make the day exciting.
One day, the old school bell
across the street became inviting.

Atop the double story school
a bell was in it's tower.
We had never heard it ring
but felt it's latent power.

Imagining the beauty of
it's vibrant, clanging song,
we sneaked in through the school-house floor,
knowing we were wrong

to go against our Grandma's words,
"Do not go in that school."
But, oh that bell had cast its spell
and we began to drool.

To find a way to make it ring;
the tower door so high;
twenty feet above the stage—
if only we could fly....

One day the old school bell across the street became inviting.

Then Cousin Dick's inventive mind
conceived a perfect plan.
"Let's pile up tables, desks and things,"
and so we all began.

To make a pyramid of all
the stuff that we could pack.
It didn't take us long to make
a wobbly looking stack.

Cousin Dick began the climb up tables, desks and such.

Lattice panels from the stage
were placed on top the pile
and through the door below the bell…
we began to smile.

A rope was hanging from the bell
down to the trap door hole.
We boosted Randy up our pile of things.
It was our goal

to tie another rope onto the
one tied to the bell
so it would reach down to the stage,
but Randy almost fell.

So Cousin Dick began the climb
up tables, desks and such.
We tried to brace his risky climb
but didn't help him much.

Then he somehow reached the top,
up through the hole he swung.
He tied the ropes together; now
that bell would soon be rung.

He gave the rope a weighty pull!!!
He tugged with all his might!!!
But when we heard that piercing DONG
we realized with fright,

that everyone within a mile
could hear that clanging bell;
that we'd better run and hide
so no one else could tell

who did the deed; who pulled the rope.
Our cousin fairly fell
as down that pile of stuff he slid
away from that old bell.

We scurried back across the road
to Grandma's house and hid,
'til Grandma called us in
and said she knew just what we did.

Dick crawled under Grandma's house; he said he wouldn't play.

She scolded us; embarrassed Dick,
for leading us astray.
Then Dick crawled under Grandma's house,
he said he wouldn't play;

he'd hide down there forever,
yes, forever there he'd stay.
We crawled in to entice him out,
but he growled—"Go Away!"

We sadly thought, that dusty place
where chickens fluffed and laid
their eggs among the spiderwebs.
we were so afraid

our Cousin Dick would soon be soiled
and he'd be thirsty too.
We thought about the frigid nights
he'd spend with naught to do.

In tears, we both sought Grandma's help,
"What should we do?" we cried.
"Just leave him be, for he'll come
out for supper," she replied.

And sure enough, when supper's smells
came wafting through the air,
our Cousin Dick just changed his mind;
he crawled right out of there.

No word was said, no story told,
about our escapades.
No one chided, no one mentioned
how a school bell bade

Young boys to scheme and plan and climb,
but never, never tell
just who it was that summer day,
that rang the old school bell.

Note: After this poem was published the first time in "The Rutabaga Patch", Walter Wilder read it and called Rex. He, as a young boy was playing outside one summer about 60 years ago at his home at Porter Creek and heard the bell rung once and stop.

He finally knew why.

SPREADING CHESTNUT WISDOM

Where are the horses, hot with sweat, that rested 'neath my wings?

The ropes that dangled from my arms to make the children's swings?

Where is the house whose big front door I watched from day to day,

as people, yes, my family, came out to work and play?

My butt is broad, it's five feet through there just above the ground.

My arms are like huge tentacles that wave and wind around.

And though I once stood in a yard where flowers 'round me bloomed,

I now am standing all alone. I miss their sweet perfume.

I must have known a hundred springs, yes even more, I guess;

my life juice surging through my veins to make a leafy dress.

And though I'm old for a chestnut tree, I feel the breath of youth,

as warm spring rains caress new leaves, they energize and soothe.

I feel alone. How have I lived beyond my normal years?
The family, the house, is gone. Now, no one prunes and shears
my limbs. They grow without restraint in grotesque, ugly shapes.
Still, passersby are beauty awed when snow my branches drapes.
And then when fall envelops me I get the urge of birth,
my verdant growth of chestnut pods illuminates my worth.

My branches creak when cold winds blow and though my skin is thick,
I suffer from an old disease that makes me rather sick.
My pods don't form the three big nuts, as in my younger days,
and no one picks them anymore except the squirrels and Jays.

But I'm alive! I'm standing tall; much taller than before!
My arms are spreading wider now. All seasons change decor.
Some say I've grown more stately, and more beautiful with age.
In winter, summer, spring, or fall, my colors draw front-page.

And there is something else I watch, just over by the road,
I have three offspring standing there. They change this episode.
A good example I must be, so they can view me proud.
I'll not complain to them of life, my head must not be bowed
until my Maker calls to me, "It's time for you to go."
Then I will pack my trunk with joy, and let the cold winds blow.

A BLOSSOM OF SPRING

A blossom is surely *a delicate thing;*
a sensitive harbinger looking for spring.
Its petals are packed in a bud on a stem
'til they burst from their prison, a colorful gem.
Encouraged by sunlight, it beckons the bees
as they search for sweet nectar in flowers and trees.

A blossom is awesome, a beautiful sight.
In sunlight exploding, then hiding at night.
When Jack Frost approaches it cowers with fear.
In heavy cold rains it sheds many-a-tear.
When blustery winds blow its petals apart,
it sighs and it cries, and exposes its heart.

The life of a blossom is measured in hours,
for under its beauty it's swelling with powers,
developing into a fluff or a fruit,
or a seed, or a pod, or a life giving shoot.

It is borne of a thought of a flower or tree
that bursts with a passion and felicity.
Precursor of fruit and a herald of spring;
a blossom *may not be a delicate thing.*

ART OF LIFE, DANCE OF PEACE

Graceful is the dance when love and peace abide.
It is not by chance all family members tried
to make the music last, to stretch the end of day.
The rhythms slow and fast were in their minds to stay.
The children learned their parts with prompting from adults,
while dancing warmed their hearts with peaceful life results.
It was a dance of peace, a form of love and art;
all tensions did release as each one did his part.
There never is an end when children early know
the dance of peace transcends all evil here below.

THE MISTIC MEADOW

The mist is on the meadow
as I gaze through early dawn.
The harvest moon is sinking
in the west, it's almost gone.
How beautiful the picture, I
see through windowpane,
my misty morning magic
waiting for the sun's refrain.

That fog is like a blanket
as it lays 'tween grass and sky.
Crawling slowly upward,
kissing tree tops on the fly.
Suddenly it dissipates
as sunlight's beams explode,
and now it merges into day
like melting a la mode.

COMING HOME

Villanelle #2

My Love, I'm coming home to you.
Can you feel my racing heart
o'er miles of green and blue?

The clouds divide and let us through.
It seems as if they fall apart,
my Love, I'm coming home to you.

I know, to me, you have been true.
The touching warmth, the teardrops start,
o'er miles of green and blue.

And through the clouds I catch a view
of home! Framed by Our Father's art.
My Love, I'm coming home to you.

We'll soon embrace as lovers do.
What ecstasy of thought; Sweetheart,
o'er miles of green and blue.

My bursting love I can't subdue!
From you I'll never more depart.
My Love I'm coming home to you
o'er miles of green and blue.

IN MY HEART I'M DANCING

Old Father Time had come to me
"to visit", so he said.
I must admit I didn't see
a reason, so I fled;

avoided him, and bid him leave,
"I haven't time," I vowed.
but he was mean, with no reprieve;
said I was not allowed
to dictate to him what I thought,
that I, no power had.
That he would simply "call the shots"
for me, though they be bad.

But I was not to be denied,
my angels hovered 'round.
They propped me up; said we would hide
from the one who wished me bound.

They loved and cared; protected me,
and gave me peace of mind.
Old father Time, no match was he,
for angels wise and kind.
A power struggle was employed
a stand-off did ensue.
Old Father Time became annoyed
at things he couldn't do.

He couldn't win my heart and mind,
but dancing he controlled.
It's hard to hear, I'm partly blind,
but I do not feel old.

I feel God's love exalting me.
My doubts and pains depart.
And though my body isn't free
I'm dancing in my heart.